ALCOHOL
AND
DRUGS
Issues
in the
Workplace

ALCOHOL AND DRUGS

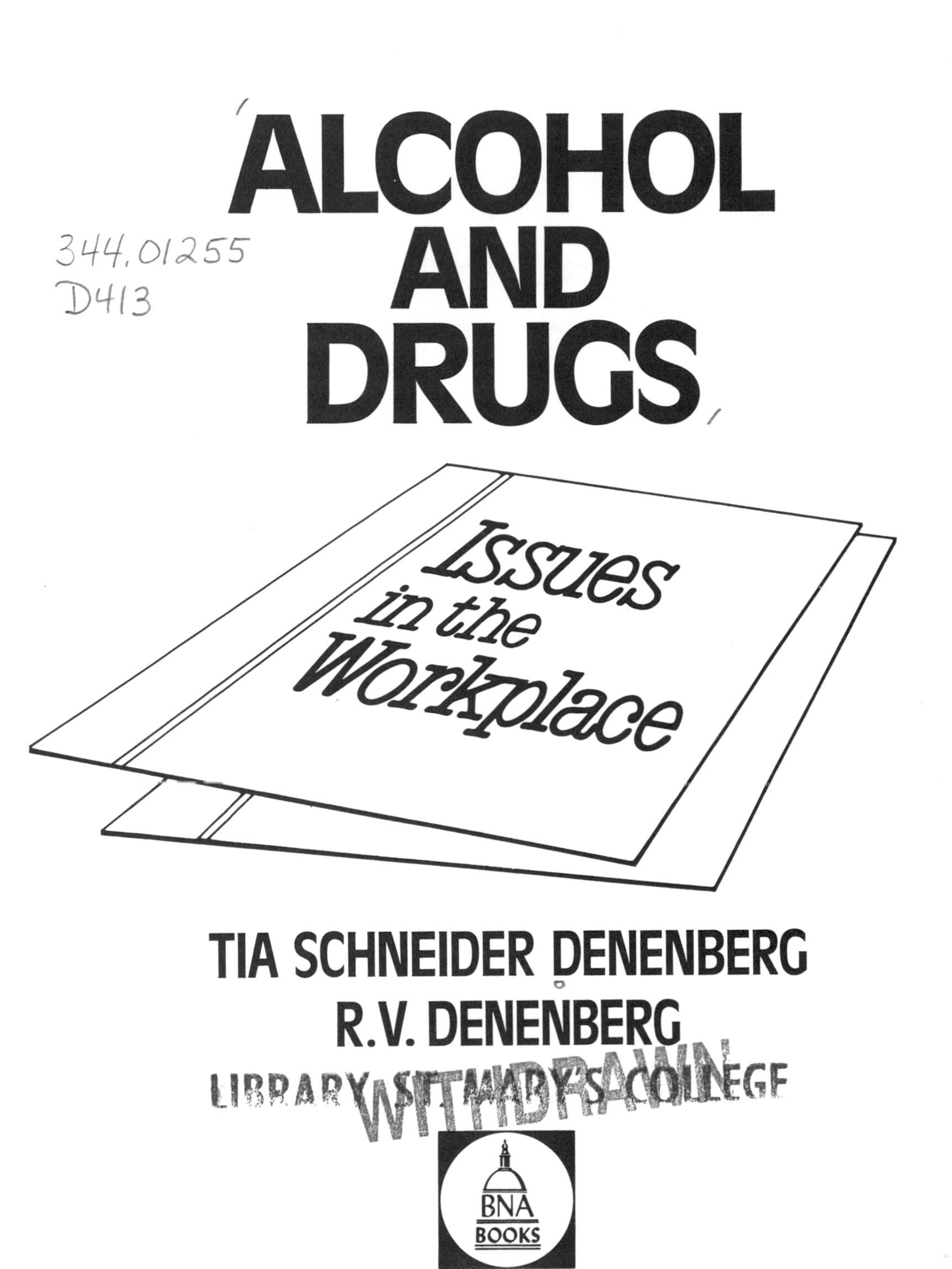

Issues in the Workplace

TIA SCHNEIDER DENENBERG
R.V. DENENBERG

BNA BOOKS

The Bureau of National Affairs, Inc. Washington, D.C.

Second Printing October 1984

Library of Congress Cataloging in Publication Data

Denenberg, Tia Schneider, 1946–
Alcohol and drugs.

Includes index.
1. Labor discipline—Law and legislation—United States. 2. Employee assistance programs—United States. 3. Alcoholism and employment—United States. 4. Drugs and employment—United States. I. Denenberg, R. V., 1942– . [DNLM: 1. Alcoholism. 2. Substance abuse. 3. Personnel management. 4. Occupational health services. WM 270 D392a]
KF3540.D46 1983 344.73′01255 83-7560
ISBN 0-87179-410-1 347.3041255

Printed in the United States of America
International Standard Book Number: 0-87179-410-1

Preface

This book is intended to meet the need for a full discussion of the important industrial relations issues raised by the impact of alcohol and drugs upon the workplace. The effects of chemical dependency require no documentation here. The economic damage in terms of lost productivity and medical expenditures is enormous: more than $100 billion annually, according to some estimates. The careers of millions of American workers are jeopardized—and often prematurely ended. Alcoholism is by no means a new menace,[1] but added to it in recent decades has been drug abuse of epidemic proportions, which seems to be growing worse.

Since an employee's involvement with alcohol or drugs frequently surfaces in a dispute over a disciplinary penalty or a discharge, it would seem prudent for industrial relations practitioners to be acquainted with the often complex issues that are peculiar to such a dispute. To those practitioners—arbitrators, representatives of employers and unions, and attorneys for both sides—this book is addressed. It is also addressed to employee assistance counselors, substance abuse specialists, and occupational medicine experts, who frequently play a part in disputes related to alcohol or drugs. Normally, each of these professionals views the problem in his own way; this book will have achieved a large part of its goal if the various segments of the industrial community are led to adopt a coordinated approach.

Because arbitrators' opinions are the culmination of actual disputes, they form a primary source for the discussion in this book. The industrial relations issues are analyzed within the context of the modern understanding of alcohol and drugs. Much about the subject is obviously still unknown; an important object of this book is to help ensure that arbitrators' decisions—and decisions made by the parties before the arbitration stage of a dispute—are founded upon what *is* known.

Few issues divide industrial relations practitioners as sharply as those related to alcohol and drugs, mirroring to some degree the divisions in society as a whole. In cases involving alcoholism, the arbitrator often faces a dilemma because conduct which by normal standards deserves corrective discipline may result from a condition which by clinical standards warrants therapeutic intervention. The proper relationship between discipline and therapy, between punishment for misconduct and treatment for an affliction, needs to be carefully defined.

In many cases, an employee's inappropriate use of alcohol or drugs does not entail alcoholism or true dependency. A single instance of intoxication or drug abuse need not mean that an employee is an alcoholic or an "addict." Nevertheless, such incidents often present unique issues—for example, the interpretation of technical evidence relating to pharmacology and physiology.

Many of the questions touched upon in these pages are opened for discussion rather than answered definitively. The opinions quoted in the text are not offered for their value as precedents—precedent, strictly speaking, does not bind arbitrators in any event—nor are they necessarily held up as models to be emulated. Instead, they are presented for their insights into the reasoning of decisionmakers as they grapple with perplexing phenomena.

It should become apparent in reading these opinions that alcohol and drug cases highlight the importance of an arbitral process which works to improve the relationship of the parties rather than to sharpen adversarial positions. The cases underscore the call by Eva Robins, in her presidential address to the 1981 meeting of the National Academy of Arbitrators, for more recognition of "the very substantial difference between the arbitration of labor disputes and litigation," in the latter of which there is "greater emphasis on winning and less on [the] obligation to the continuing relationships."[2]

The cases also are powerful—and often disturbing—reminders that arbitration properly should be a last resort in the settlement of labor-management disputes. No matter how wise, an arbitrator is unlikely to produce a result as satisfactory as that which could flow from early joint intervention by the parties themselves when alcohol or drug problems arise. By the time the arbitration stage of a dispute is reached, the safety and productivity of the workplace may have been seriously jeopardized, and the chances of aiding an employee suffering from alcoholism or drug abuse may have been drastically diminished.

The authors have attempted to keep the organization of the book straightforward. Some chapters deal exclusively with drugs or alcohol; others focus on issues pertaining to both substances. The first chapter is concerned with disciplinary infractions by employees who are regarded as alcoholics. The second chapter discusses discipline or discharge for conduct related to drugs. Chapter Three details the impact of an Employee Assistance Program on the handling of cases which involve either alcohol or drugs, and Chapter Four analyzes the standards of proof and evidence appropriate to both types of cases. Chapter Five takes up the medical and technical questions often presented by alcohol cases, and Chapter Six does the same for drug cases. In the seventh and eighth chapters the application of employer rules and the impact of the collective bargaining agreement respectively are examined in relation to both alcohol and drugs. The dominant themes of the book are reviewed in the conclusion, which is followed by a series of reference appendices. They include a case-finder chart that guides the reader—under 40 subject headings—to alcohol and drug cases published by The Bureau of National Affairs, Inc. in the *Labor Arbitration Reports.* These cases are cited by volume and page, *e.g.*, 50 LA 173. The use of "he" and "his" in general discussions in this book should be understood to be a shortened form of "he or she" and "his or her." Obviously individuals of both sexes are involved in all aspects of the subject dealt with here.

The title of the first chapter is adapted from that of a seminal paper by Gerald Somers, presented to another, earlier meeting of the National Academy of Arbitrators.[3] Each of us in the field of arbitration owes a debt of gratitude to Professor Somers for warning that "alcoholism in industry poses serious problems not only for the alcoholic employee, his company and his union, but also for the enlightened arbitrator." Sadly, Professor Somers' work was cut short by his untimely death. This book, it is hoped, will help extend life—the working lives of those whose careers are threatened by alcohol and drugs.

Acknowledgments

A number of persons have given the authors the benefit of their experience in a variety of fields related to this book, and we are indebted to them for their advice, suggestions and comments. Although the responsibility for any errors or omissions is the authors' alone, we wish to note that John Williamson, Industrial Relations Manager, and Sylvia G. Rennicke, Administrator of the Employee Assistance Program at the Carpenter Technology Corporation, were invaluable sounding boards, as were Richard L. Masters, M.D., Aeromedical Advisor of the Air Line Pilots Association; Carl J. Schramm, Director of the Center for Hospital Finance and Management, Johns Hopkins Medical Institutions; James R. Merikangas, M.D., Assistant Clinical Professor of Psychiatry at the Yale University School of Medicine; and Judith S. Stern, Professor of Nutrition, University of California, Davis.

Many arbitrators were generous with their time and case materials. Eva Robins and Helen M. Witt provided detailed, insightful comments on early drafts of the manuscript, and materials supplied by Alfred C. Dybeck, Richard Mittenthal and Marian Kincaid Warns enlarged the perspective of the book. Helpful comments also came from Frances Bairstow, Dana E. Eischen, Margery F. Gootnick, Marcia L. Greenbaum and James and Fritzi Sherman. James C. Hill graciously gave us the use of his personal library.

Much information about alcohol and drugs was supplied by William S. Dunkin, Director of Labor–Management Services at the National Council on Alcoholism; Thomas J. Delaney, Jr., Executive Director of the Association of Labor–Management Administrators and Consultants on Alcoholism, Inc.; John Quinn and William R. Byers of the New York State Division of Alcoholism and Alcohol Abuse (Occupational/Industrial Bureau); David L. Diamond, Associate Attorney of the New York State Division of Substance Abuse Services; and John V. Howland, Director of Community Relations at the Arms Acres treatment facility in Carmel, New York.

Gordon Law, Reference Librarian at the Cornell University School of Industrial and Labor Relations, kindly gave us access to the school's outstanding collection. Research material also came from arbitrators, employers, unions, academics and treatment specialists. Although they are too numerous to name, we extend our thanks for their vital contribution.

The research for this book began when the authors worked with Susann Malin of the American Arbitration Association to organize a conference on arbitration of drug and alcohol cases, which was held in New York in April 1980. Steve Silvia of Cornell University and Susan Mackenzie, arbitrator, helped gather case materials for the conference that were ultimately incorporated in the charts in Appendix E of this book. Stephen Price of Vassar College compiled the case data in a computer-readable format. John Bradley, assisted by Richard Klein, both of Cornell University, checked the charts. Clerical assistance was provided by Lillian and Sidney Schneider and Edith Platt.

T. S. D.
R. V. D.

Jackson Corners, N.Y.
June 1983

Contents

Tables

1

Alcoholism and Just Cause for Discharge

Approaches to Alcoholism

Alcoholism in the workplace causes alarming economic loss and personal tragedy. Employees in all categories—from the shop floor to the executive suite—have proven susceptible to alcoholism, whose manifestations include poor job performance, absenteeism, lateness, erratic behavior and excessive use of medical benefits. In many industries it is often left to an arbitrator to decide how to deal with an employee whose work has been affected by alcohol. Yet there is a great divergence of views in the arbitration community about precisely what alcoholism is and what approach should be taken with those who suffer from it.

Some consider alcoholism an illness, albeit a complex one with physiological and mental components. Two main views have been discerned within this group, the physical and the psychological:

The Physical View

The view that prevails in lay as well as professional circles is the physical view, the "disease concept of alcoholism," formulated originally by Dr. E. M. Jellinek, a pioneer in the field of alcohol studies. This concept may be explained as follows:

> Some people—the people who become alcoholics—are born with a specific physical vulnerability to the physiological effects of alcohol. Because of this vulnerability, their reaction to alcohol is more intense than that of others and they develop a much greater need for alcohol than others, a need

> that becomes an obsession and ultimately an addiction.
>
> . . .
>
> The disease lies dormant, so to speak, until the susceptible individual begins to drink. Then a predetermined, predictable process is initiated.

The Psychological View

The concept of alcoholism as a psychological problem is, essentially, expressed as follows:

> People who become alcoholics are alcoholism-prone, not because of a physical disability, but because of psychological disabilities. These are people who, in childhood, went through disturbing emotional experiences such as rejection by parents, parental cruelty, inability to make friends, lack of success in school, lack of fulfillment and gratification, constant parental conflict, alcoholism in the family, a broken home, among other difficulties. As a result of such distressing experiences, these children developed feelings of anxiety, insecurity, depression, loneliness, repressed anger, low self-esteem—feelings they carry into their adolescence and adult life.
>
> . . .
>
> Persons so predisposed have an urgent need for (1) relief from emotional distress; (2) an easy, instant source of pleasure, gratification, and self-esteem; (3) a way to deal with a reality they cannot handle. Alcohol provides all of these. It anesthetizes emotional pain, produces euphoria, inflates the deflated ego, beautifies the ugly self-image, and modifies reality so the drinker does not have to deal with it.
>
> Dependence on alcohol for these effects is at first limited, but it expands, crowding out realistic alternatives until, eventually, it dominates the personality entirely.[1]

Others, however, seem reluctant to draw a close analogy between alcoholism and illness, primarily because they are unwilling to disregard what they consider an element of personal responsibility. Alcoholics, to these people, are "weak-willed" and lacking in self-discipline. They would, to varying degrees, hold alcoholics accountable for their condition in a way that they would not hold diabetics or cardiac patients accountable. Indeed, alcoholism is surely the only disorder whose typical manifestation—intoxication—is sometimes specified in collective bargaining agreements as a cause for summary discharge.

Complicating the nature of alcoholism is that not everyone who becomes intoxicated, even repeatedly, is an alcoholic. As the Federal Aviation Administration has stated in its guidelines for airline employees, "there is often some justifiable confusion in differentiating between alcohol abuse and alcoholism."[2]

Three Models in Arbitration

Attitudes toward alcoholism influence the approach used in deciding specific cases. Three main schools of thought concerning the proper approach to take are discernible among arbitrators:

1) *Straightforward application of the traditional corrective discipline model.* Employees are judged solely on the basis of their performance on the job without regard to clinical explanations of their shortcomings. Discharges even of those suffering from alcoholism are upheld so long as the employer has adhered to the disciplinary requirements of the collective bargaining agreement.

2) *Rejection of the corrective discipline model in favor of a therapeutic model.* The alcoholic employee is deemed to be the victim of a disorder and is offered opportunities to recover, including leaves of absence and appropriate treatment. Repeat offenses are not necessarily regarded as cause for increasingly severe penalties but as perhaps inevitable slips on the long road to recovery. Failure implies the need for more treatment, not more punishment.

(3) *Modification of the corrective discipline model.* This middle-ground approach operates on the theory that the employee suffers from an illness but ultimately may be subject to discharge, perhaps after being given one "second chance," and allows for some opportunity for recovery while insisting that employees remain substantially accountable for their behavior.

None of the three approaches is entirely free of difficulties, either conceptual or practical. The more closely one adheres to the corrective discipline model, the more one confronts the realization that alcoholism is often a hidden condition underlying the superficial behavior (such as tardiness or absenteeism) for which the employee ostensibly is being disciplined. This model is thus limited to grappling with surface effects rather than with underlying causes.

The therapeutic model can be difficult to apply because techniques for treating alcoholism vary considerably and are still being developed. Broadly speaking, they include drug therapy, psychotherapy, behavior therapy and eclectic therapy; this last technique utilizes a variety of individual and group counseling activities.[3] The prognosis in each case, as well as the length of time needed for therapy, is uncertain. Even those who are most successful in treatment may speak of themselves as "recovering" rather than "recovered" alcoholics, because treatment success is typically measured by the alcoholic's ability to maintain total abstinence.[4]

The middle-ground approach also is not trouble free, inasmuch as it tries to combine two often immiscible elements—punishment and treatment. To the extent that the two cannot be reconciled, the arbitrator may be faced with a choice between finding the grievant culpable or finding him treatable.

Alcoholism as a Mitigating Factor

The variety of approaches has produced a plethora of specific issues on which there seems to be little settled opinion. Prominent among these issues is the extent to which alcoholism may be a mitigating factor in an evaluation of the conduct or performance for which an employee has been discharged.

In the absence of an explicit contractual provision or well-established practice, some arbitrators have been unwilling to allow any departures from standard discipline on the grounds of alcoholism alone. The following excerpts are illustrative of this line of arbitral reasoning:

> There is no dispute that grievant was guilty of excessive absenteeism and that if he had been a normal healthy individual the company would have cause to discharge him. [Would] the fact that he was a confirmed alcoholic, which fact was . . . not . . . made known to the company until after his discharge, be sufficient to extend to him amnesty from his excessive absenteeism?
>
> . . . Nowhere in the currently effective collective bargaining agreement or company rules is there any provision granting amnesty for chronic alcoholism or sickness from enforcement of company rules concerning excessive absenteeism. It is clear that the company gave grievant appropriate warnings that his continued excessive absenteeism would result in his discharge. It also complied with the progressive steps of discipline outlined in its rules, and further, went beyond the bounds of cause for discharge as provided by the bargaining agreement by granting him a "last chance" probation the union proposed, which grievant

ultimately violated with full knowledge that it would result in his discharge. Even after discharge the company extended the grievant's hospital insurance at its own expense although not obligated to do so . . . . It would seem justifiable that the company not be penalized for its voluntary humanitarian actions.[5]

* * * * *

I deny the grievance and uphold the discharge with certainty but without any sense of accomplishment. [The grievant] was clearly a good worker and an attribute to the company and the union when he was not drinking.[6]

Other arbitrators, however, are willing to give an employee the benefit of the doubt if the discharge resulted from alcoholism. They are inclined to reinstate the alcoholic whenever there seems to be a possibility of recovery. These are typical rationales:

We all share a moral obligation toward those less blessed than ourselves to make a maximum effort to help them enter and stay in the mainstream of American life . . . . The arbitrator . . . feels that the grievant is salvageable. One more chance is in order.[7]

* * * * *

In the arbitrator's judgement, the positive factors concerning the grievant at this point in his travail outweigh the negative factors. The grievant should be given yet another opportunity to demonstrate that he has managed to acquire an acceptable control over his problem. He has assured the arbitrator that he understands the rigorous necessity for abstinence.[8]

* * * * *

There can be no doubt that the company followed its regular procedure to the letter in arriving at discharge as punishment for the offense. No step was omitted. It made sure that the evidence was complete. It gave repeated warnings. It imposed progressively more severe punishments. Its actions were impeccable except in one respect. The punishment imposed showed concern for the employer's welfare but not enough for the employee's. The punishment was applied mechanically without sufficient regard for the circumstances surrounding the event and the individual.

. . .

Of course, an employer is not required to put up with an alcoholic indefinitely but this does not mean that an alcoholic is to be treated as a pariah and shunned without further responsibility.

> The employer owes an employee, especially an honorable and long-standing employee, the obligation of making at least one attempt to get him to rehabilitate himself.[9]

Second Chances

Paradoxically, the value of "second chances" is often challenged by treatment specialists, who point out that a symptom of alcoholism is "denial," the adamant refusal of alcoholics to recognize their condition. In some instances, it is argued, alcoholic employees may construe a second chance as a vindication of their denial—with predictably disastrous results. The discouraging corollary is that in many cases only through losing their jobs are alcoholics shocked into confronting reality, a phenomenon sometimes ironically referred to as "dismissal therapy."

Unless treatment is administered, Professors Harrison M. Trice and James A. Belasco have argued, "the employee, even if reinstated, is likely to continue his behavior and is just as likely to be discharged again,"[10] a result which generally "adds approximately 2½ years to the period of time during which the employer must absorb the economic costs of a problem employee."[11]

The futility of many reinstatements is confirmed by a study of several hundred discharge cases, involving a variety of offenses, conducted by Professor George W. Adams. He found:

> Those employees who were fired for intoxication and absenteeism had the poorest performance records subsequent to reinstatement. Experience with intoxication supports the conclusion of other studies that, regardless of seniority, the chronic absentee or alcoholic is likely to be discharged a second time.
>
> Alcohol cases stand out, attracting subsequent discharges in 50 percent of the cases—the highest post-reinstatement discharge rate of all offense categories—and recurring discipline was necessary in a further 20 percent. Thus, the offense with one of the highest rates of reinstatement had the least successful reinstatement experience.[12]

It is far from clear, however, that reinstatement can never lead to recovery and that an employee must actually be out on the street before he can begin transforming himself. Some authorities on alcoholism maintain that the mere threat of losing one's job can become part of what Professor Trice and Professor Paul M. Roman have called a "constructive confrontation strategy" for "bringing about a job-related crisis in the deviant drinker's life while he still holds a job."[13] This strategy presumes that the alcoholic's job is such an important facet of his self-esteem that the very prospect of its loss will force him to seek treatment. According to one study of industrial treatment programs:

> The "crisis" . . . which confrontation at work precipitates is unlike the crisis of sudden status loss which students of the skid row alcoholic tell us will lead the suddenly fired alcoholic, for example, to cushion his loss by association with similar (alcoholic) status losers . . . . Rather, it is the *threat of loss* of existing social position, self-respect and other intangibles that go with employment.[14]

The confrontation must be accompanied by constructive assistance in the form of therapy and counseling, for, as Professors Trice and Belasco point out:

> Since there is nothing in the corrective discipline procedure, as such, to deal with the basic causes of the employee's deviation, corrective discipline alone merely generates a job-related crisis for the emotionally disturbed employee without offering him a way out of the crisis.
>
> . . . Without the offer of treatment and the positive effort to get the alcoholic or emotionally disturbed employee to undergo treatment, discipline will probably have little or no effect.[15]

Implications for the Arbitrator

What this means for the arbitrator is that a "second chance," to be effective, ought to be viewed as part of the therapeutic crisis in which the grievant is led to accept treatment as the price of reinstatement. The alternative often is merely a grim series of arbitrations, extending over many years, in which the employee is reinstated several times before he is confronted with the hard choice of making progress toward recovery or losing his job. In some of these sagas, the employee is able to prevail by persuading various arbitrators that the type of therapy chosen for him was inappropriate, the company was insensitive to his needs or his rights had been violated in other ways. In the short term, such decisions may seem benevolent. In the long run, the delay in facing up to the difficulties of recovery may amount to a form of "coffin lining," in the parlance of the therapists: arbitrators become "enablers" who make it possible for the grievant to go on drinking, and each arbitration is only an episode in a long career of alcoholism.

Indeed, an arbitration may be the fruit of an alcoholic employee's attempt to exploit union–management differences for his own ends. As one researcher has observed: "Many [occupational alcoholism counselors] contend that the alcoholic worker is a manipulative person who will attempt to pit union against management in order to avoid the consequences of his or her problem. If this is the case, an adversary relation between union and management can play right into the alcoholic employee's strategy."[16]

Andy Y.: A Case Study

What follows is an actual case history of one employee, "Andy Y." Employed by a steel company since 1959, his "therapeutic crisis" did not occur until 1982, although he had been discharged three times before. The first time was in 1967, when his disciplinary record was as follows:

1/15/62	Unacceptable grinding job	1-day suspension
5/04/62	Unacceptable grinding job	1-day suspension
10/09/63	Unacceptable grinding job	1-day suspension
1/10/64	Unacceptable grinding job	1-day suspension
5/25/64	Reporting late for work	Written warning
4/09/65	Lateness	Written warning
11/02/65	Not reporting lateness and unacceptable excuse	Written warning
9/13/67	Defective work	Written warning
11/07/67 (last day worked, 10/3/67)	Violation of company rules	Discharged

The violation concerned a company rule against gambling. Andy was one of several employees with whom Pinkerton undercover agents had placed numbers, football or horse-racing bets. All grievants were reinstated, but without back pay, by the arbitrator, who saw "no evidence . . . that any of the grievants have unsatisfactory records of service" or that they "were king-pins or the chief entrepreneurs of any gambling enterprises."

It is not clear whether Andy's alcohol problem had already begun by then, but after being reinstated in December 1967, he proceeded to compile the following record:

6/11/68	Sleeping in locker room	Written warning
5/13/70	Tardiness	Written warning
8/27/75	Tardiness	Written warning
12/05/75	Tardiness	Written warning
4/14/76	Unfit for work and insubordination	1-day suspension
2/28/78	Unfit for work and insubordination	1-day suspension
6/26/78	Unfit to work	3-day suspension; Final Warning
12/02/78	Reporting to work in an unfit condition	5-day suspension; termination to follow

Second Arbitration

When Andy's future with the company was again at stake in an arbitration, he was a self-acknowledged alcoholic. An important aspect of the union's argument on his behalf was that Andy had been treated unfairly by the company's employee assistance coordinator, who had tried to get him into treatment when he had been suspended for three days about six months before the discharge. The coordinator tried unsuccessfully to have Andy enter "a private detoxification and psychological center for alcoholics [for 21 to 28 days], plus attendance each Sunday night at the A.A. [Alcoholics Anonymous] meeting held at the plant and weekly attendance at . . . two other, outside A.A. meetings." Andy refused the inpatient treatment program for "several good reasons," including a visit from a crippled sister (he was the only one who could carry her from her car to his house), the loss of earnings during the period that he would be an inpatient, and the fact that "physically he felt fine and did not believe that several days of detoxification were necessary." The grievant testified that the counselor had rejected these reasons as spurious.

The union's position was that the coordinator was unqualified to make what it considered to be a mandatory treatment determination, and the union noted that Andy had voluntarily joined AA after rejecting the counselor's all-or-nothing approach. The arbitrator ruled for the grievant, faulting the counselor for ignoring "the value of an individualized approach to the alcoholic and his problems." The arbitrator concluded that Andy's "refusal to accept in June 1978 the [inpatient treatment] offer colored the objectivity of the final review of his case in December . . . and leaves a doubt in the arbitrator's mind as to the fairness of the December decision to terminate." Andy was reinstated unconditionally but without back pay in April 1979.

He did not continue attending AA meetings, and he was again terminated for being unfit a year later. However, the company's practice was not to call attention in an arbitration to past discipline if the employee had a clean record for a year. (He exceeded the year by about three days.) Therefore, the discharge never went to arbitration; the company agreed to reinstatement without back pay on the understanding that it constituted a last chance for Andy. Informally, the union undertook to persuade him to enter an alcohol treatment program, although no conditions were attached to his reinstatement.

Andy's list of infractions, however, continued to grow:

3/20/80	Operating machine in an improper manner	Written warning
4/25/80	Improper conduct	Written warning
10/23/80	Poor job performance	Written warning
11/07/80	Leaving department and plant without permission	Written warning
2/16/81	Tardiness	Verbal warning
3/13/81	Leaving safety chain off the coolant pit	Verbal warning
3/26/82	Unfit condition while working	5-day suspension; termination to follow

Alcoholism Confronted

In April 1982 this discharge went to the third-step grievance meeting, after which the company reinstated Andy Y. on the condition that "he agrees to and fulfills conditions established to direct him to and maintain him on a path of recovery" since Andy

> now recognizes that he suffers from alcoholism, that he cannot maintain recovery from his alcoholism by his own resources, and that he is willing to enter into the company's Employee Assistance Program in order to recover.
>
> [Andy's] service of over 22 years with the company and his willingness to work whenever the company requests his services speak in his favor. However, he must realize that there must be a limit to the patience of his supervision and the company in tolerating his instances of reporting to or being at work in an unfit condition. That patience is at the breaking point.

Andy entered into a detailed "last chance" agreement and a program agreement (see "Last Chance Agreements" in Chapter 8) in which he acknowledged his alcoholism and finally accepted the company's offer of treatment. Ironically, the program began with inpatient treatment similar to that which he had, for "good reasons," rejected four years earlier, and it was arranged by the same Employee Assistance Program coordinator.

The tortuous and sad story of Andy Y., who went through four discharges and two arbitrations before confronting his alcoholism, underscores the futility of reinstatement unaccompanied by an effort to deal with the underlying condition. Although it was in everyone's interest that the therapeutic crisis occur much earlier, the reinstatements—particularly those of 1979 and 1980—merely allowed Andy to drink for a few more years. A turning point occurred only after his last discharge, when his union decided to support the effort to get Andy into residential treatment.

The Andy Y. case study also points out that arbitration, which prides itself on its finality, may be just an incident in a protracted dispute over an alcoholic employee. One reason for the lack of a decisive outcome is that arbitration tends to focus on relatively narrow issues and to regard reinstatement as a resolution when, of course, it may resolve little.

Medical Leave and Conditional Reinstatement: The Second Chance

A course adopted by some arbitrators in cases like Andy Y.'s has been to convert a discharge to a mandatory medical leave of absence, during which the grievant is to seek treatment. The grievant's reinstatement is deferred until he is medically certified as fit to return to work. It has been argued that

> where probable cause exists for concluding that an employee's misconduct was due to alcohol or drug addiction, there is an indicated necessity for a psychiatric or psychological or medical evaluation.
>
> Should the medical report . . . state conclusively that the employee's misconduct is caused by addiction, justice and fairness require conversion of the dismissal into a one-year paid and/or unpaid leave of absence. The arbitrator might well retain jurisdiction for that year to permit psychiatric examination, if requested. Should a later determination show rehabilitation, the award could provide for automatic reinstatement.[17]

There are some serious drawbacks to imposing medical leaves as a method of dealing with the alcoholic employee. As a practical matter, recovery is a continuous process, rendering uncertain the point at which the grievant could justifiably be declared rehabilitated. Determining the precise moment when he is sufficiently recovered to work may entail a second arbitration or force the arbitrator to retain jurisdiction indefinitely (see Chapter 3). Moreover, many treatment specialists believe it unwise for arbitration to focus upon the alcoholic's condition rather than his job performance.

Another common solution is to reduce the discharge to conditional reinstatement. The extent to which the arbitrator properly may set the conditions is open to question, in terms of both the therapeutic process and the arbitration process. On occasion arbitrators have gone so far as to recommend the medicine (Antabuse) the grievant was to take. An experienced occupational alcoholism specialist has observed: "Some of the cases . . . suggest that arbitrators are making or interpreting clinical decisions—i.e., whether a person is an alcoholic or how long he should be treated. These are clinical decisions that should be left to clinicians."[18]

Curtailing Procedural Rights

Most arbitrators refrain from turning their award sheets into prescription pads, but some are willing to curtail the grievant's prospective procedural rights as a *quid pro quo* for reinstatement. In a typical award of this type, an employee was required to commit herself in advance to taking medical tests:

> 1. The grievant . . . shall, accordingly, be reinstated without back pay . . . on the following conditions:

a. That if she is found drinking any alcoholic beverage on the job she shall be immediately discharged.
b. That she shall sign, and submit a copy to the arbitrator, the employer and the union, authorization for the hospital to administer an appropriate test for alcohol whenever the grievant's supervisors have reasonable cause to believe that she may be under the influence of alcohol on the job.

. . .

d. Should the grievant refuse to take such a test, it shall be presumed that she is inebriated and she shall be discharged immediately.

2. In order to assure a swift and efficient resolution of any problems which may arise, the arbitrator retains jurisdiction of this dispute until the expiration of the current agreement between the parties.[19]

It can be argued fairly that awards which leave the grievant shorn of normal rights enjoyed by other workers under the agreement may exceed the scope of the arbitrator's authority and impose an unfair burden on the employee, who is, after all, presumed to be suffering from a disorder. Such a remedy, moreover, shows little of the faith in ultimate recovery which led the arbitrator to opt for reinstatement in the first place.

Other Alternatives

A more straightforward, and less onerous, variant of the conditional reinstatement may be framed in terms such as these:

> The grievant must be reinstated by the employer at such time as the employee satisfactorily demonstrates that:
> 1. He has undertaken treatment . . . through a responsible treatment center or program.
> 2. His participation in such a program is being maintained on a continuing basis.
>
> Failure on the part of the grievant to attempt to resolve his drinking problem in this manner negates his reinstatement.[20]

Here, the reinstatement focuses not on fixing the date of recovery but on good faith effort toward recovery, and it preserves normal procedural rights. Another variant, in the case of an employee who has refused assistance for alcoholism in the past, is to issue an award which offers the employee a choice between immediate termination and making a commitment to recovery. For example, a rubber worker with 10 years seniority was discharged for repeatedly failing to report impending absences. He acknowledged that his poor record was due to alcoholism, but he had in the past rebuffed offers of assistance for his condition. An arbitrator offered him the following options:

> 1. [The grievant] shall be reinstated to his former job and classification with full seniority but no back pay [for 30 days]. . . . The company, the union and the grievant shall mutually agree on a formalized program into which the grievant shall enroll for treatment. Weekly reports shall be sent to the company and the union indicating whether or not [the grievant] has fulfilled his commitment to the program. At the end of the 30-day period, the company at its discretion shall reinstate the grievant to full employment or terminate him finally depending upon an equitable and fair examination of the reports and documentation furnished to them, and [the grievant's] own attitude.
>
> Or alternatively,
>
> 2. If the grievant does not want to commit to the 30-day treatment and surveillance, his termination shall be upheld as of [the date of discharge].[21]

Health Benefits

An important factor in fashioning conditional reinstatements that call for treatment is the scope of the employer's health benefits program. Before about 1970, most group insurance plans did not provide payments for alcoholism treatment, partly for cost-containment reasons and partly because of a belief that alcoholism was self-induced. Since then many insurers have instituted coverage for alcoholism treatment, deciding that it is less costly than paying for the medical complications of advanced alcoholism, such as cirrhosis. However, the extent of reimbursement varies widely. A survey of more than 300 employers taken by the Conference Board, a management research organization, found that nearly all of them provided insurance coverage for hospital inpatient treatment for alcoholism but that less than two-thirds offered coverage for a residential alcoholism treatment facility. (The cost of a typical stay in such a facility amounts to thousands of dollars.) Paid leave to attend treatment was also far from universal.[22]

Post-Discharge Behavior

In arbitration there is generally a well-accepted principle that the employee's post-discharge behavior has no bearing on whether the employer had just cause for the discharge. As one arbitrator observed, "The only relevant evidence are the facts which the person making the discharge was in possession of at the time he acted."[23]

In alcohol cases, however, arbitrators often have been willing to take into account evidence that an employee has brought under control the drinking behavior which led to the discharge. The considerations which led to this departure were summarized as follows:

> [T]he evidence shows clearly that *since* he was discharged, grievant has done the sort of things that an alcoholic should do. He placed himself under the care of his physician. He joined Alcoholics Anonymous, and has regularly attended its sessions. He has taken help from a church, and from an alcoholic treatment center. . . . Representatives of those agencies and his doctor have issued written statements to the effect that he is doing well. No contradictory evidence was submitted on that point. Accordingly, the chairman concludes that grievant has been making progress on the road towards control of his addiction. In petitioning for some modification of the discharge, the union emphasizes these recent events. The corporation contends among other things that they are not relevant, and that the chairman should decide the case on the basis of the circumstances as they existed on [the discharge date].
>
> . . .
>
> The remaining question, then, is to what extent if at all such events justify modification of the grievant's discharge. The corporation argues with reason that he had ample opportunity to attempt to rehabilitate himself *before* he was discharged, and that therefore no mitigating significance should be accorded his subsequent efforts in that direction. On the other hand the union emphasized, also with reason, that one of the characteristic features of alcoholism is a psychological *inability* on the part of the person affected to face up to the rigors of rehabilitation until some drastic consequence such as discharge befalls him. Consideration of that fact, the union reasons, justified a conclusion that grievant be reinstated and reimbursed for some portion of his lost time.
>
> The close balance between those conflicting considerations is tilted slightly in grievant's favor, the chairman believes, by (a) his long seniority, (b) his reputation as a good worker, and (c) the fact that his prior conduct record is clear except for the mentioned instances of discipline for intoxication. The chairman's

> conclusion, limited of course to the particular facts of the case, is the grievant should be reinstated, but without back pay.[24]

Other arbitrators, however, have refused to make any exception in alcohol cases to the rule that post-discharge behavior is to be disregarded. An arbitrator, for example, upheld the discharge of an alcoholic employee whom he believed to be fully rehabilitated by the time the arbitration took place. He found:

> It is the grievant's condition and conduct at the time of his discharge which must be the sole determinant, not [his condition] at some later date.

However, like many other arbitrators, torn between traditional arbitral procedure and an obviously changed grievant, he also offered a nonbinding recommendation in favor of the grievant's reinstatement:

> Of course, the arbitrator has no right to order the company to reinstate or rehire the grievant . . . but in the interest of the fine work done by AA, coupled with the display of courage and will power by the grievant to help himself, and his ability to make his rehabilitation "stick" the company might well consider the possibility of giving him "a break" if it can use his abilities on a job opening. The arbitrator well recognizes that this may be construed by some as a "hearts and flowers" appeal, but in the interest of helping to "lick" the growing problem of alcoholism in industry [the arbitrator] is willing "to stick his neck out" in making the suggestion. He is tremendously interested in seeing the alcoholic problem solved, but realizes it takes the combined efforts of the individual employee, the company, the union, the community, and the fine organization Alcoholics Anonymous to place rehabilitants in jobs, so that they may not lose their courage to go straight because they find the door to job opportunities closed to them.[25]

A similar nonbinding recommendation was offered by another arbitrator:

> [The company] cites the following controlling contract clause in the instant case:
>
> "8. Bringing or consuming alcoholic beverages or narcotics onto plant premises shall subject the employee to immediate discharge."
>
> . . . The company submits that the arbitrator has no choice but to sustain the discharge. . . .
>
> . . . [T]he penalty, having been discussed at length and mutually agreed to, can hardly be modified by the arbitrator . . . .

> However, I do believe the company should take another look at its position. In this country today alcoholism has become recognized as a "sickness." The grievant, following his discharge, had himself admitted to the . . . hospital for two weeks, and then spent a week at the . . . rehabilitation center. At the hearing, he testified that he had joined Alcoholics Anonymous and had not taken a drink since his discharge.
>
> While your arbitrator cannot rule that C., 45 years of age with almost five years of continuous service with the company, be given a "second chance," I would certainly recommend it.[26]

Motivation

In deciding whether to grant a second chance, arbitrators appear to make an assessment of the employee's motivation for recovery. There is some evidence, though, that employees who are coerced into treatment programs are as successful as those who enter voluntarily. A review of a number of treatment programs concluded:

> Historically, the position of many alcoholism therapists has been to regard the voluntary seeking by the alcoholic of treatment as an indicator of "patient motivation" and thereby an important factor in treatment success. . . . [But] studies of the chronic public inebriate show that coercive or nonvoluntary referral to treatment is not necessarily an obstacle to treatment participation and success. . . . The evidence from industrial alcoholism programs similarly favors coercive referrals.[27]

This is not to say that motivation should be disregarded, but it should be borne in mind that the unwilling as well as the willing may benefit from treatment programs once exposed to them.

2

Arbitrating Employee Drug Abuse Cases

Drug Abuse as a Treatable Disorder

Although the notion of alcoholism as a treatable disorder is gaining ground among industrial relations decisionmakers, there seems to be much more resistance to the concept of rehabilitating an employee who is drug-dependent. Several reasons might be adduced to explain this resistance. To begin with, alcoholism is a much more familiar disorder than drug abuse, which became widespread only in recent decades. Second, some drugs, such as marijuana, have been primarily associated with the youngest members of the workforce, whereas management and union leaders (and arbitrators) are generally more senior and perhaps therefore less sympathetic—although prescription drug abuse seems to be no respecter of age categories. Finally, some drug involvements carry a taint of criminality, leading industrial relations decisionmakers to view the problem as one of law enforcement rather than therapy.

From a scientific standpoint, abuse of alcohol and abuse of other substances have much in common. The American Psychiatric Association has created a general diagnostic category entitled "Substance Use Disorders," defined as behavioral changes caused by alcohol, barbiturates and similar sedatives and hypnotics, opioids, amphetamines or cannabis (marijuana). Characterizing the disorders may be any or all of the following: "impairment in social or occupational functioning . . . , inability to control use of or to stop taking the substance, and the development of serious withdrawal symptoms after cessation of or reduction in substance use."[1]

Some researchers have argued that, from the standpoint of physiological effects, the abuse of drugs is not qualitatively different from the abuse of alcohol. A study of drug abuse commissioned by the Ford Foundation concluded that

> the common distinction between alcohol and "drugs of abuse" is based on the fact that alcohol is known and accepted in the culture, not on any pharmacological considerations. It is entirely possible that alcohol is inherently more dangerous than most of the other drugs.

The study goes on to report the conclusion of one authority that alcohol ranks third among hazardous drugs, well ahead of heroin and LSD.[2]

That view has received some support from industrial medicine specialists. Dr. Robert P. Jessup, an aerospace industry medical director, has noted that the "employee who smokes pot at lunch sees no difference between himself and his co-worker who may have two martinis for lunch. A confirmed marijuana smoker, if need arises, can come down off his high and function. This is something he likes to point out that his drinking co-worker cannot do."[3] Moreover, there are corporate medical directors who believe that the standard governing drug use as well as alcohol use should be job performance. An insurance industry medical director, Dr. John B. Cromie, has argued that the "question of whether the identification or diagnosis of drug abusers is synonymous with termination of employment must be answered with an emphatic no. If the individual is doing his job, I do not believe that any company has the right to fire him."[4]

The Legal Status of Abused Drugs

It is universally recognized, nevertheless, that a drug used by an employee can differ from alcohol in one highly significant respect: the drug may be illegal. This is not true, of course, of all abused substances. Employees may be abusing lawfully obtained prescription drugs or over-the-counter drugs for which no prescription is needed. Medication is frequently misused by being taken in too large or too frequent doses or by being combined with alcohol. This is particularly true of tranquilizers like

Valium and Quaalude and a number of other psychoactive prescription drugs (see "Proving Impairment by Drugs" in Chapter 6). They may also be abusing a substance which is not technically a drug or medicine at all, as in the case of glue sniffing.[5] But in many arbitration cases, the grievant is involved with the so-called "street drugs," such as heroin, whose possession, sale and use are prohibited by federal and state laws. Or a grievant may be accused of using other federally controlled substances, such as prescription drugs which have bona fide medical applications but were obtained illegally and administered without medical authorization—drugs such as amphetamines, anti-anxiety agents (tranquilizers) and barbiturates.

One issue before the arbitrator, then, is the extent to which the legal status of the drug should affect the outcome of the case. There is some evidence that the taint of criminality weighs heavily in the decisionmaking process. A survey of 87 arbitrators showed that the "hardness" or "softness" of the drug in question would affect their decision of a case. The "hard" drugs, particularly heroin and other opium derivatives, are all substances whose possession, sale and use carry heavy penalties under federal and state laws. Marijuana tended to be considered a "soft" drug, apparently because, although still illicit, the trend of legislation at the time of the survey, the mid-1970s, had been toward reduction of penalties for personal possession and use.[6]

Decriminalization and Discipline

In specific cases, however, arbitrators have disagreed about the extent to which "decriminalization" should affect the employer's ability to impose discipline upon an employee involved with marijuana. Here are three arbitral views:

> It is true that marijuana's long-term effect on humans is still disputed by the experts, but most seem to agree that its short-term effect varies from individual to individual. Because of its widespread use, especially by the younger age group, some jurisdictions in this country . . . have decriminalized the personal use of marijuana. In [the state where the case arose], however, it is still a criminal offense and offenders may be fined, imprisoned, or both. The arbitrator, therefore, finds that the five-day suspension is reasonable and not "too steep" as charged by the grievant.[7]

* * * * *

The arbitrator is mindful that there is a growing tolerance of marijuana, and that there may be further decriminalization. But at this point the arbitrator cannot very well say the company did not have proper cause to discharge the grievant merely because it does not choose to adopt a permissive view of grievant's conduct. Since the arbitrator has concluded that grievant was in possession of marijuana and furnished it to a fellow employee at work, the company was within its contractual rights in discharging the grievant.[8]

* * * * *

In the performance of his duty, the arbitrator, as well as the courts, must look into the factual situation which exists in light of today's knowledge. Laws, like customs and mores, do not rest in a vacuum, isolated and unresponsive to the needs of an ever-changing society . . . . This arbitrator therefore has an obligation to examine the effect of recent legislation in determining the propriety of grievant's discharge for an illegal act, for it is precisely the illegality of the use of marijuana that separates this violation from the use of alcohol, fighting on the job or insubordination.

. . .

. . . [T]he arbitrator does not here decide that because of the decriminalization of the use of less than an ounce of marijuana under [state] law the company does not have the right to discharge an employee for engaging in this conduct. On the contrary, the company's right to discharge for marijuana use is fully recognized. However, the arbitrator does find that the company has the responsibility to consider this factor, i.e., the decriminalization, as well as the employee's overall record and his length of service in determining the appropriateness of the penalty.

. . .

. . . [T]his arbitrator must conclude that although the grievant clearly violated the company rule concerning use of marijuana, the company's summary discharge was not for just and sufficient cause.[9]

Although during the 1970s 11 states decriminalized marijuana possession for personal use by substituting small fines for jail terms, the trend may have reached its peak. A report by the National Academy of Sciences in 1982 found that the drug posed physical and emotional dangers sufficient to cause "serious national concern."[10] Much of the concern has been focused on increasing evidence of regular use by persons as young as 14 or 15. In addition, the marijuana now being used in the United States—much of it domestically grown by a thriving industry of "green-collar workers"—is said to be of a more potent variety than that which was previously available. Proposals to remove all criminal penalties for personal marijuana use have been firmly rejected by federal health officials. To the extent that arbitrators have taken into account community mores, this subtle shift away from relaxation of penalties may influence the outcome of discipline cases.

Drug Involvement in the Workplace

On-duty use, possession or distribution of a drug affords a surer ground for employee discipline than off-duty involvement; the presence of drugs in the workplace could lead to accidents and loss of productivity, and it may make the employer's premises a locus of criminal activity.

In many instances, an employee who is discovered to be involved with drugs in the workplace is summarily discharged. Industrial "capital punishment" for such offenses is warranted by the enormity of the offense, employers typically argue. There may be, however, no contractual provision or company rule explicitly prohibiting drugs or setting forth penalties for their use. Summary discharge, moreover, may conflict with contractual requirements for progressive discipline, including the issuing of warnings and graduated penalties.

Arbitrators differ about whether an employee may be summarily discharged for on-duty involvement with a drug—even if illegal—in the absence of a clearly promulgated contract provision or company rule. Consider these two opinions:

> [T]he union contends that since the plant rules are a part of the contract, and since the company contracted for progressive discipline for such serious offenses as drinking on the job, working while intoxicated, etc., puffing on two marijuana cigarettes should not be considered as anything more than a single major offense, to be punished as a first offense, by a three day suspension.
>
> The vice with the union's argument is that the first offense of possession of marijuana is a crime in [the state], punishable by a fine of $500 and imprisonment for six months, and subsequent offenses are felonies subject to increasingly severe punishment . . . while public drunkenness per se is not a crime . . . .
>
> I sanction the discharge from employment in this case on the ground that it is an implied condition of any collective bargaining agreement that, unless specifically stated to the contrary, there are some offenses which are so great that discharge from employment is the only appropriate penalty.[11]

* * * * *

> [I]n the absence of such prior rule [against marijuana] with notice of the penalty for its violation, the arbitrator does not believe that any disciplinary action is proper in this case which would be in excess of what the shop rules contemplated for the possession of alcohol.
>
> Therefore, the arbitrator finds and concludes that D——'s discharge was not warranted under the facts . . . and the circumstances then existing and that the penalty of discharge should be reduced to what it would have been for the first violation of the rule relating to the possession of or drinking of any alcoholic beverage on company property, namely, a written warning with a three-day suspension.[12]

An important consideration is whether the employer was attempting to deal with acknowledged drug use in the plant. Arbitrators have shown an unwillingness to overrule summary discharges imposed as part of a campaign to combat drug use among employees, even when the contract might be interpreted as requiring progressive discipline. In one case an arbitrator upheld the discharge without warning of four employees for using or making available to other employees marijuana and the hallucinogens mescaline and "angel dust" (PCP or phencyclidine) on company premises. Company investigators had identified the four after officials received complaints from other employees that drugs were being used. The union argued that the penalty violated a contractual provision requiring at least one disciplinary warning except for discharges for "dishonesty, drunkenness or recklessness resulting in an accident while on duty." The arbitrator rejected the argument:

> The company here had a recognized serious problem with respect to drug use and abuse among its employees . . . . Its premises were being used for the commission of crimes condemned by the statutes of the state . . . . To follow the literal wording of the contract that a warning is necessary in all cases except a few enumerated situations . . . would permit the grievants to avail themselves of the legalistic language for the purpose of working an injustice on the company and possible injury resulting from drug abuse.
>
> . . .
>
> The company should not be "hamstrung" in its attempt to eradicate a serious condition which could create safety hazards. To permit these grievants or other employees to believe that they can indulge in the use of drugs while at work or commit crimes on company property and not impair their right to employment unless they are first warned goes beyond that which the parties contemplated when they wrote the contract language with respect to progressive discipline. The legal right to have a warning

before discharge has to give way to the greater equity right of the company not to be subjected to an injustice because of agreed-to language.[13]

Arrest, Indictment and Conviction

Arbitrators generally are reluctant to sustain disciplinary charges based upon incidents that did not occur in the work place, but exceptions are made when the employer can show that the off-duty conduct adversely affected his business or reputation, threatened the welfare or morale of other employees or rendered the grievant unfit to perform his duties. An employee's off-duty involvement with drugs often gives rise to just such concerns. A person who uses or sells drugs may be considered an accident and health risk to himself and others in the workplace—and a potential source of crime. When an employee is arrested or indicted on drug charges, does an employer have grounds for disciplinary measures? Arbitrators evidently disagree. Here are two examples of arbitral reasoning:

> Obviously, indictment on a criminal charge [of possessing and selling marijuana] is not the same as being guilty of the charge, and for many criminal indictments there would not exist a justification for the company to suspend an employee or take other disciplinary action against him until after he had been found guilty. However, the seriousness of the drug problem and the need for an employer to strive to prevent any drug abuse among its employees would warrant a finding that a company has the right to act immediately to protect its own interests and the interests of its employees.[14]

* * * * *

> The eight days grievant missed within a two week span . . . were largely beyond his control, since he had to appear in court and then went to jail when he was unsuccessful in raising bond . . . .
>
> . . .
>
> The offense for which the grievant was imprisoned [possession of narcotics] occurred outside the plant. So far as the record shows, the grievant's problem has not been a threat to his fellow employees. The arbitrator would not, for one instant, deny the company the right to protect its force from exposure to drug traffic. The union has assured the arbitrator that it would not support anyone who represented a potentially harmful influence on its members at this plant, in such a dangerous way. The grievant

seemed to recognize the error of having any connection with drugs . . . .

Everything considered, it is the arbitrator's conclusion that the absences shown in this record, taking into account their involuntary nature, were not sufficient to warrant the extreme penalty of discharge.[15]

Railroad Industry Practices

In the railroad industry, merely being charged with a drug offense has been held to be sufficient to sustain a dismissal where the employee's resulting incarceration prevented him from reporting for duty when on call. A Public Law Board, for example, denied the grievance of a trainman–yardman who was discharged after being jailed in lieu of bond on a charge of delivering a controlled narcotic substance, a charge to which he ultimately pled guilty. The board held:

> [The grievant's] guilt on the drug charge was not proven at or prior to the [employer's] investigation[;] thus he was entitled to a presumption of innocence at such time. Nevertheless, we find that proof of missing a call while incarcerated in jail is just cause for discharge in the absence of proof of innocence by the employee. The burden shifted to [the grievant], and, of course, he was unable to sustain the burden.[16]

The same board upheld a discharge of a trainman for "conduct unbecoming an employee" after he was jailed for possession of cannabis, reckless driving and leaving the scene of an accident. The grievant had been involved in several automobile accidents, at the last of which he "got out of his car and disposed of a substantial amount of marijuana and other illicit drugs." The board wrote:

> The original incident received considerable public attention, and we agree with [the railroad's] position that in a city the size of Galesburg [Illinois] the incident would subject [the railroad] to justified criticism, particularly if [the railroad] had kept [the grievant] on its payroll. Moving trains are instruments of death, and no railroad can afford to condone the use of, or trafficking in, illicit drugs.[17]

Indictment *Versus* Conviction

A practical rule of thumb is that mere indictment, as opposed to conviction, gives the employer narrower grounds for fearing danger to the work environment. A discharge is more easily sustained when the employee has been convicted, especially if the offense is not merely possession but trafficking, for the employer can argue that drug sales to other employees must be prevented. In a typical case, several grievants were suspended when they were indicted on drug charges, and one was discharged after being convicted of selling marijuana to an undercover policeman. The arbitrator, upholding the discharge as well as the suspensions, wrote:

> [H]owever tolerant society may be towards personal possession and use of marijuana by individuals, there is no indication that such tolerance extends to individuals who engage in the sale of the substance for profit. This is shown in the current trend in state laws which set for possession only a considerably lesser penalty for that offense as against the sale of marijuana . . . .
>
> Furthermore, what studies have been made indicate that a person, who will use marijuana, will not necessarily become a user of hard drugs. On the other hand, there is no evidence available to indicate that persons, who would sell marijuana for profit, will necessarily limit themselves solely to that product, and will not also satisfy the demands of other customers for the more dangerous drugs, if and when the opportunities to do so arise. For such reasons the conclusion must be reached that possession of marijuana for purposes of sale for profit constitutes a far more serious violation than mere possession and use.
>
> . . .
>
> The nature of drug sales is such that [they are] not easily detected, and to require that a company cannot act against employees, who engage in the sale of illegal drugs for profit, unless it catches them in the act on company property, would deny to the company the power to police successfully its work force either to prevent the creation of a drug problem among its employees or to combat effectively an existing problem that may have arisen.[18]

In a similar case, a grievant, while on sick leave, had delivered about 30 grams of marijuana—a felony under state law—to an undercover policeman. The grievant's sentence permitted him release time to work at his job, but the employer discharged him. Upholding the discharge, the arbitrator wrote:

> One engaged in selling drugs for profit is already beyond the law. The profit motive will be a strong incentive to expand the market and broaden the product line. Few, if any, drug dealers could be caught if they refrained from selling to unknown customers. Opportunity for profit led the grievant to deliver drugs to an unknown undercover agent. An even stronger incentive

would exist to sell to those well-known, such as fellow employees. The same disregard for law would permit rather than limit sales on company property.[19]

In another case, the grievant was discharged after being convicted and imprisoned on charges of trafficking in cocaine. Since he was on layoff status, he lost no work time and sought to overturn the discharge on the grounds that the incident was insufficiently work related. The arbitrator ruled for the employer, finding that management had a right to act to protect employee safety:

> [T]he distinction between use of and trafficking in drugs is important in an employment context; the person engaged in the latter type of conduct is involved in activity for profit that can result in slipshod work performance by those employees who might purchase the drugs from him. The peddler need not be a user himself, but that in no way diminishes the danger that his activity creates for the users or those persons associated with such users; indeed, the danger increases, for drug control or rehabilitation programs are of no rehabilitative value to the peddler.[20]

Effects on Employees

The guiding principle here appears to be the effects on other employees. Where the grievant has been convicted of an offense involving selling drugs, the import for fellow employees is clear. But the effect of simple drug use or off-site possession on an employee's coworkers is not as direct, unless the assumption is valid that an off-duty user is inevitably an on-duty user or a conduit for drugs to enter the plant and become available to coworkers. That a worker has been convicted of possessing drugs in his home, for example, may not give the employer a substantial reason to believe that he possesses or uses them at work. Morever, as some arbitrators have held, possession itself does not necessarily demonstrate use and is a lesser offense than use. Consider these two rulings:

> Even when the necessity of deterring other company employees from misconduct is given full weight, I find myself unable to agree that the grievant's first offense of possession of the illegal amphetamine pill under the circumstances of this case was such as to render the discharge penalty fair or just. I am distinguishing the mere fact of possession alone of a single pill from trafficking in or use of illegal drugs during working hours or on company premises.[21]

* * * * *

> Had the evidence in the instant case established the grievant [convicted of possession of amphetamines] to be a drug user, the arbitrator would sustain the discharge without hesitation. Without minimizing the seriousness of the grievant's misdemeanor conviction for possession, it is the arbitrator's opinion that his offense should not be bracketed with the felony crimes of "narcotics addiction" or "forcible rape." Nor is there any basis for assuming a comparable impact upon the work force.[22]

Criminal Charges *Versus* Discharge

The disposition of the criminal charges *per se* is not always the controlling factor in a discharge arbitration. The evidence against an arrested employee may be insufficient in a criminal case, or the prosecution may be flawed by defective warrants or other technical imperfections. But the case against the employee still may be convincing enough to justify action by the employer.

That is particularly true where the employer might suffer loss of public confidence as a result of the employee's involvement with drugs. This consideration was the heart of a case involving an auxiliary police officer:

> [T]he arbitration forum deals with industrial jurisprudence in accordance with its own rules and standards which are not necessarily the standards which obtain in other forums, including courts. Thus, an employee found guilty of some cause in court might be held completely free of work liability in arbitration. Conversely, an employee found not guilty in a court might be deemed accountable industrial-relations-wise, on the same count. In this matter, the grievant was not even determined to be *not guilty* by the court. The charge was dismissed *without prejudice* and without consideration of the merits on technical grounds and does not at all obviate the requirement that *merits* must be considered in this arbitration.
>
> . . .
>
> The grievant was, in fact, an auxiliary member of the police force . . . . Consequently, this episode reflects adversely against the reputation of the . . . police force, if countenanced, and could induce:
>
> a. shattered morale among the officers, or
> b. contempt for necessity to practice conformance with the laws among all city employees.[23]

However, there may be situations in which the charges

themselves are the only real indication that the employer has of employee wrongdoing, so that, if they are dropped, no cause for discipline exists. In a case involving marijuana charges, an arbitrator wrote:

> [O]nce the company knew the charges had been dismissed . . . , justice required reinstatement at that point in time. No significant continuing damage to the company could then be assumed as likely. To disagree is to assume that the public does not believe in American judicial philosophy. It follows that the discharge became unjust and improper . . . on . . . the date of dismissed charges. While it is possible that charges may be reinstituted, or that the grievant may violate a plant rule in the future, such contingency cannot be allowed to outweigh the certainty of adverse employment effect on the grievant now and later.[24]

When criminal charges are pending against the grievant, the arbitration may become a kind of mini-trial of the allegations soon to be tried in court. In one case, the employer attempted to convince an arbitration board that it had just cause for discharging the grievant, who had been arrested but not yet tried for feloniously possessing 40 pounds of marijuana at his home. The arresting officer was called as a witness. The board concluded:

> Since the grievant has never been convicted of the felony alleged, the company assumed the full burden of proving same in this matter . . . .
>
> On the record at hand, the board is unable to find clear and convincing evidence of grievant's alleged wrongdoing. Thus, the discharge cannot stand. If the grievant is hereafter convicted pursuant to the criminal charge now pending, then this may raise some new and different issues which have not been presented to or decided by this board.[25]

Rehabilitating Drug Abusers

In general, arbitrators have been reluctant to overturn discharges for drug use on the ground that the employee should have been offered a chance for rehabilitation. This may be a reflection, as we have seen above, of the general reluctance throughout the arbitration community to regard drug addiction as a treatable disorder. However, some arbitrators have drawn the line at discharging an employee *because* he was a drug user undergoing rehabilitation.

In one case, an employer discharged a mill janitor when it discovered that he was receiving daily doses of methadone, which blocks the action of heroin. A posted plant rule stated: "Any employee found possessing, dispensing, using or under the influence of any drug on company premises without proper authorization from the company's medical department is subject to discharge." The company maintained that methadone, like heroin, is an addictive narcotic which impairs the user's reactions and judgment, and that the same reasons which justify discharging a heroin user justify discharging a methadone user.

After reviewing considerable medical evidence about methadone, the arbitrator rejected the company's contention:

> Management is within its rights in barring a heroin addict from the plant. A true addict is unfit for employment. He requires heroin at least once a day and often more than that. His reaction to the drug initially is euphoria, then drowsiness, then a period of relative "normality," and finally withdrawal symptoms. Because heroin is not long-lasting, a fix may give an addict no more than a six- to eight-hour respite. He then is hungry for the next fix. This endless craving for heroin dominates his day, his every thought. Most experts seem to agree that addicts in such a state are functionally disabled . . . .
>
> . . .
>
> This case concerns an employee addict who had stopped taking heroin and who was instead enrolled in a state-sponsored drug rehabilitation program which provided him with a daily dosage of methadone and whatever counseling and therapy he needed.
>
> . . .
>
> . . . [T]he controlled use of methadone does not cause a euphoric reaction. It appears too that once the body develops a methadone tolerance, the drug does not mask pain or cause drowsiness. Because methadone is long-lasting and is taken daily, there is no problem with withdrawal symptoms. And there is no craving for the drug. Thus, the disabilities of heroin are simply not present in methadone maintenance.
>
> . . .
>
> Given these circumstances, the company's position in this case must be rejected. It would be wrong to rule that an employee on a methadone maintenance program can be discharged because he is taking an addictive narcotic. The evidence indicates that his controlled use of methadone has practically no adverse effect upon him. His reactions, judgment, perception, and so on are not impaired. He can, particularly in the case of a mill janitor, . . . perform his work safely and effectively.

The arbitrator did, however, acknowledge that "there is sharp disagreement in the medical community as to the wisdom and effectiveness of using methadone as a means of treating heroin addiction," because the maintenance program typically must be carried on indefinitely. And he cautioned that in reinstating the grievant he was not deciding "the question of whether an employee on methadone maintenance should be permitted to run a crane or perform other work which calls for quick and sure reactions."[26]

When the grievant reported to the plant for his reemployment physical, a urine sample revealed the presence not only of methadone but also of morphine, a metabolite of heroin. He was again discharged, this time for "failure to abide by the proscription of the methadone maintenance program which provided the basis for [his] reinstatement under [the preceding] award."

The case came before the same arbitrator, who once more reinstated the grievant with full back pay:

> The dispute . . . boils down to an evaluation of [grievant's] performance in the methadone maintenance program. To begin with, neither [of the centers treating the grievant] expect[s] addicts in the program to be completely free of drug abuse. They realize that the addict in the initial weeks of treatment will frequently take heroin to test the efficacy of methadone, i.e., to see whether methadone blocks the effects of heroin. They realize that an occasional reversion to heroin or some other hard drug will occur with many addicts, particularly when exposed to anxieties and tensions they are unable to handle. [Grievant's counselor] testified that one such "dirty" urine every four months was permissible. In his opinion, such a result with a "hard core" addict like [the grievant] is a success because the pattern of addiction has been broken and the occasional use of heroin is the exception rather than the rule.

The grievant provided the center "with a urine sample, each Monday through Friday, before he gets his methadone." The arbitrator was given a record of these tests over an extensive period of time and concluded that the grievant

> was taking heroin during his first two weeks in the program . . . . That . . . is not at all unusual . . . . [F]or the next ten months, [grievant] had a fairly good record. He took heroin just twice . . . . Apart from these two slips, his urine sample almost always revealed just methadone . . . . [Several months after his discharge he] had a serious slip . . . when he took heroin for several weeks.

> . . .
>
> When one examines [grievant's] record in light of the realities of a drug rehabilitation program, it is not at all bad as the company asserts . . . . He is still a part of the program and he is still receiving his daily dosage of methadone . . . . [H]is counselor has high hopes for him.
>
> For all these reasons, I find that the evidence does not establish that [grievant] "fail[ed] to abide by the proscription of the Methadone Maintenance Program." His occasional use of heroin, given the circumstances of this case, does not prove noncompliance with the drug rehabilitation program.[27]

Effects of Rehabilitation Programs

Incentive to Discharge Traffickers

Where they exist, drug rehabilitation programs may be an alternative to discharge. But such a program may also give an added incentive for discharging employees who sell drugs; an employer may argue that these employees are a menace to coworkers attempting to shake the drug habit. Taking note of an employer's efforts at drug rehabilitation, an arbitrator wrote:

> Whether out of altruism, or a means to reduce accidents and absenteeism, or for other reasons, the company has invested time and money to develop and implement a drug rehabilitation program. The purpose of this program is to provide aid to those employees seeking help with a problem that they can't handle . . . .
>
> . . . Prevention may well be the chief means of making a sound rehabilitation program truly effective. In an attempt to apply the element of prevention to the program, the company has taken the position that an employee convicted of selling drugs will be discharged . . . . The company's position in this matter, that the return of the grievant to the work force could do serious damage to this new and needed program, is neither unreasonable or unsound.[28]

Remand to Program as Mitigating Circumstance

That a drug-using employee was sent by the law enforcement authorities to a rehabilitation program rather than prosecuted can amount to mitigating circumstances in a discharge. A supermarket employee who was arrested for possessing amphetamines (he used them while at work) was reinstated in part because

> [H]is arrest did not lead to a trial and conviction but to submission to a "diversionary program" used by the authorities to divert first offenders from habitual use of drugs. He has been rehabilitated and this should be considered in favor of his attempt to return to his job, particularly since this is his first offense.[29]

Similarly, a grant of probation to a drug offender so that he may reform himself can militate against a discharge based upon the conviction. An employee who pled guilty to a charge of possession of marijuana was reinstated, in part because the court placed him on probation. The arbitrator reasoned:

> [T]he judicial authority of the state has determined that the proper corrective measures to be applied are to free grievant under suitable restrictions and supervision rather than to incarcerate him. This determination was presumably based upon a comprehensive investigation, evaluation and recommendation conducted by the probation department . . . .
>
> Having . . . initially elected to base its decision to discharge upon the judgment of the court, the company now stands on the bare fact of conviction and closes its eyes to the grant of probation. The grant of probation was an inseparable element of the conviction; it represents a determination that grievant is a safe and useful member of society with the assistance of the probation department.[30]

In a related case, a grievant who had been arrested for possession of marijuana was reinstated after being placed on probation:

> This incident was [the grievant's] first offense. [Next month], provided he is not rearrested, his criminal court case will be dismissed, rendering the entire criminal case a nullity. If the judicial system sees fit to give the grievant an opportunity to continue his life with an unblemished record we conclude that we should do the same. Justice without mercy is not justice.[31]

Conditional Reinstatement

Arbitrators have also fashioned a kind of probationary status for marijuana offenders by offering them conditional reinstatement. In one case, the arbitrator imposed the following detailed conditions:

> The reinstatement is conditional, i.e.,
>
> a. if the grievant is found to possess marijuana on company property, the company is free to discharge him at will.
> b. if the grievant is again found guilty of selling or buying

marijuana outside the company premises by a court, the company is free to discharge at will.

c. for . . . three calendar years . . . the grievant's absenteeism and lateness are subject to the following rules . . . .
   a. for a second lateness, a suspension of five work days; for a fourth lateness, an additional suspension of 10 work days; for a sixth lateness, discharge.
   b. after two unexcused absences, the company is free to discharge at will.
   c. the grievant hereby loses all further protection under the just cause provision of the contract in criminal matters, absenteeism, and tardiness.[32]

Conditional reinstatements in drug cases no doubt should be approached with the same reservations as conditional reinstatements in alcohol cases (discussed in "Medical Leave and Conditional Reinstatement: The Second Chance" in Chapter 1). There is, of course, a great deal of difference between a marijuana user and an alcoholic. A marijuana smoker may be using the substance as a "recreational drug" (see "Classifying Drugs" in Chapter 6) and may not suffer from habituation. On the other hand, there may be substantial psychic dependence, requiring treatment. In any event, the nature of the drug use should clearly figure in the fashioning of the reinstatement remedy.

3

Arbitration and the Employee Assistance Program

The Employer's Obligation "To Be of Help"

Although some observers have discerned the emergence of a concept that every employer has a duty to assist alcoholics and drug addicts,[1] the primary instrument for dealing with these problems has been the voluntarily created Employee Assistance Program (EAP), run by an employer or a union or as a joint effort. In a historical study, Harrison M. Trice and Monica Schonbrunn traced "the roots of job-based alcoholism programs . . . back to the late 19th–early 20th century efforts by employers to eliminate the long-accepted use of alcohol in the workplace." They wrote:

> Three forces combined in the late thirties and during the war years to escalate these concerns into embryonic programs. These were the rapid rise of Alcoholics Anonymous, the sudden and enlarged need for workers during the war, and the concern of industrial physicians. . . . The "keep it quiet" theme of the early forties rapidly gave way to more open publicity in the latter part of the decade. . . . By the mid-fifties there were full blown efforts underway in at least fifty or sixty companies and unions.[2]

A 1982 study by former Secretary of Health, Education and Welfare Joseph Califano found that the "growth of EAPs has been impressive during the 1970s" but that as yet only 12 percent of the nation's workforce, primarily employees of large companies, had access to them. Still, the accomplishments of EAPs so far have been encouraging. The Califano study noted that "reported recovery rates for alcoholics referred to treatment through EAPs range as high as 90 percent, and in any good program they should be above 50 percent." A General Motors program, for example, provided assistance from 1972 to 1979 to more than 42,000 workers, most of them afflicted with alcohol problems. As a result, "time off the job declined by 40 percent and sickness and accident benefit payments dropped by 60 percent. GM also found that accidents on the job, management disciplinary actions and employee grievances were cut in half for the treated group."[3]

Although many EAPs tended initially to concentrate on alcoholism, they now typically are concerned with drugs and other health and social problems as well. An EAP does not undertake treatment itself but refers employees to the appropriate treatment facility. Often a group of smaller companies will form a consortium to run an EAP, housed in an independent center, for their combined workforce. The ideal EAP, according to the Califano report, has the support of union leaders and top managers:

> Stigma clings to alcoholism. Many employees will not voluntarily participate in an alcoholism program if the atmosphere is threatening or even ambiguous. Alcoholics and problem drinkers will not seek help where they believe that the risk to their job is greater from identifying themselves than from trying to get by without calling attention to their drinking problems.[4]

Informal peer-group programs offer one way to overcome that obstacle. An example is the Human Intervention and Motivation Study, sponsored by the Air Line Pilots Association, which has helped ALPA members with alcohol-related problems to return to duty.[5]

Rehabilitation Before Discipline?

For those involved with arbitration, the most salient question posed by the EAP movement is whether the employer who maintains or recognizes an EAP or even promulgates a policy on alcohol rehabilitation incurs an obligation to try rehabilitation before imposing discipline. Put another way, is that employer expected to detect incipient alcoholism in an employee and to offer assistance before the employee's poor performance leads to discharge?

One Company's Application of Policy

The employer's obligation was at issue in a case in which a telephone company employee was suspended and 10 days later discharged for a series of incidents of misconduct, including insubordination and absenting himself without authorization. Between the suspension and the discharge, he entered an alcoholism recovery program at a hospital to begin several months of treatment. The union maintained that his misdeeds were attributable to alcoholism—although the employee failed to raise that issue until his final suspension, pending discharge. The union argued that the discharge was not for just cause, since the company had departed from its own policy of offering to rehabilitate alcoholics.

The company's policy statement on alcoholism was indeed quite detailed. It included the following:

> POLICY
>
> Some problem drinkers may not be willing to admit that they have a problem and may refuse the services of the medical department or other rehabilitation agencies approved by the medical department. In such cases, the individual's behavior and performance must be subject to departmental disciplinary and administrative action.
>
> Employees may seek help through sources other than the company's medical department. Such programs must be made known and must be approved by the medical department.
>
> ADMINISTRATION
>
> A. *Recognition*
>
> Some of the signs which may indicate excessive drinking are listed below. These indications may be the result of other causes, so supervisors should not jump to conclusions.
>
> 1. Steadily deteriorating or inadequate work performance.
> 2. Erratic work or unfinished assignments.
> 3. Repeated absenteeism of a day or a half-day at a time, with frequent Monday, post-holiday and post-payday absences.
> 4. Temporary absences from the job or unexplained disappearances from an assignment.
> 5. An increase in minor illnesses, illness excuses or too frequent on and off the job accidents, particularly where the employee's role in the accident is difficult to identify.
> 6. Changes of mood with apparent personality changes. Disinterest in work or any marked change in disposition or appearance. Presence of hand tremors, flushed face,

red or bleary eyes, loud talking, memory gap or obvious hangovers.

7. Drinking during working hours or at lunch time.
8. Not infrequently clues may be obtained from the individual's drinking habits, e.g., heavy spending on drinking, gulping drinks down quickly or more excuses for having a drink, etc.

B. *Employee Discussion*

The supervisor should first call attention to the employee's poor job performance—being specific as to the aspects of the work which are inadequate. The employee should clearly understand that his deficient work performance must be corrected and that the supervisor wishes to help him improve.

Some of the above signs (absenteeism, erratic work, etc.) will suggest that some health problem does exist and the supervisor may therefore recommend to the employee that help be obtained from the medical department.

Specific mention of drinking or alcoholism should not be made by the supervisor unless the employee brings up the subject himself or unless there is conclusive evidence of abuse—such as drinking on the job.

When an employee, suspected of being a problem drinker, continues to perform unsatisfactorily, the supervisor should consult with higher management and then with the medical department to arrange for medical assistance. The objective at this point is to have the employee visit the medical department for a health checkup. If the employee agrees that he has developed a drinking problem, then the medical department and the employee's supervisor can work together in the rehabilitation program necessary to correct the work deficiencies.

If the employee fails to admit his drinking problem or declines assistance from the medical department or from any other recognized rehabilitation center, the supervisor should remind the employee that his job is in jeopardy. The supervisor will then follow through with disciplinary action but until such time as the employee's services are terminated the company stands ready to be of help.

The Arbitrator's Findings

The arbitrator found that the grievant had been suffering from alcoholism for some time before the final suspension and that

> his unusual behavioral symptoms for the eleven month period [before the suspension] were [classic] of alcoholics . . . . In fact, his behavior manifested nearly all of the signs of recognition contained in the company's policy statement. After eight years

> of satisfactory accomplishment, his work performance . . . steadily deteriorated; he did not complete his assignments; disappeared from his job without explanation; underwent personality changes so that he showed disinterest in his work and became resentful, boisterous and annoying. His failure to admit his alcoholism to others was also symptomatic of his condition, as again reflected by the policy statement.[6]

The arbitrator concluded that the company's intent in framing the policy statement was to show that "it stands ready and willing to assist an employee suffering from alcoholism during his employment," and he ruled that to discharge an employee after management became aware that he was an alcoholic (and that he had begun rehabilitation efforts) "does not carry out such intent."

The arbitrator was unmoved by the company's assertion that the decision to discharge the grievant had already been made at the time of the final suspension—before the employee disclosed that he was an alcoholic:

> The inclusion of a suspension period pending discharge is not unusual in labor–management contracts and often is used as a cooling off period to head off precipitous supervisors' judgments . . . . [A]n admission of alcoholism by an employee often comes after the highly traumatic experience of actual or threatened discharge from employment. When such admission occurs prior to the final termination and especially, when accompanied by solid rehabilitative efforts, it imposes a duty on management to . . . investigate . . . the genuineness of the grievant's condition and his attempts to become rehabilitated. This, seemingly, was not done in this case.[7]

The arbitrator held that the discharge was without just cause since management had failed to adhere to its own policy: the company had not met its obligation "to be of help."

Possible Burden for Progressive Employers

This decision suggests that company guidelines to supervisors encouraging them to identify alcoholics and direct them toward treatment may be interpreted as a company policy mandating attempts at treatment in *bona fide* cases of alcoholism, even where adequate grounds for discipline exist. Thus, those employers which take the initiative in attempting to deal constructively with alcoholism may bear an extra burden in arbitration not borne by less progressive employers. The implication is that employers who voluntarily institute treatment or guidance programs must exhaust the opportunities they provide for rehabilitation before turning to dismissal.

The reasons for not placing such a burden on employers are many. For one thing, it might discourage otherwise laudable attempts by employers to turn toward rehabilitation as an alternative to discipline. Moreover, since "denial" is a strong feature of the disorder, employees are likely to rebuff approaches by supervisors and coworkers, admitting to alcoholism only after discharge is imminent. Nor is it always easy to identify the symptoms. As the arbitrator in the case discussed above acknowledged:

> [I]t is significant that not only [the grievant's] supervisors but his co-workers and more especially his steward, a close colleague and friend, as well, were unable to discern his symptoms. It is not suggested that they were negligent in such respect but merely that chronic alcoholic behavior cannot easily be recognized by laymen and that the alcoholics themselves, like other neurotics, are masters at covering up their neuroses.
>
> . . .
>
> A company is not a hospital clinic for its employees. Its managers and supervisors are not expected to be capable of diagnosing physical or mental illnesses. Thus, even though the personnel policies may offer suggestions and clues for recognizing problem drinkers among employees or associates, it does not impose an affirmative duty on supervisors to identify them, and the company cannot be held responsible for the failure of supervisors to do so.[8]

In addition, the possibility should be recognized that arbitral willingness to overrule a discharge because the grievant admitted to alcoholism at the eleventh hour—when notified of an impending dismissal—may encourage other alcoholics among the employees to avoid confronting the problem at an early stage. Thus, the price of vindicating one employee's right to rehabilitation may be the prolongation of the suffering of others.

A Second Interpretation

It is noteworthy that in a subsequent case involving the same parties, the company's obligation "to be of help" was again tested, this time with different results. The case concerned a building mechanic with nine years of service who crashed the company truck he was driving into two parked cars, resulting in his arrest for driving while intoxicated. He entered an alcoholism rehabilitation center, where he remained for about three months. About 21 months later, the company reinstated him without back pay, treating the interim period as a disciplinary suspension. The grievant challenged the propriety of the discipline.

The arbitrator ruled:

> Absent a contract provision, other bilateral arrangements, or a binding practice to the contrary, an employer has the right to discharge an employee who drives a company vehicle while intoxicated and who, as a consequence, causes an accident. In that circumstance, mitigation of that penalty because the employee suffers from the disease of alcoholism is a matter within the employer's discretion and not for the arbitrator.
>
> If the employer exercises that discretion by establishing circumstances or criteria for the imposition of the penalty less than discharge, the union's right to challenge is limited to whether the circumstances and criteria are arbitrary, capricious or unreasonable and/or if those established conditions and standards are unevenhandedly or discriminatorily applied or denied to employees similarly situated.
>
> Here there is no special contract provision dealing with the matter of disciplinary penalties for an alcoholic. Nor do I find any bilaterally negotiated or agreed to arrangement or a practice of mitigation applicable to the essential facts of this case.
>
> Instead, the company has established a policy under which it will *consider* mitigating or not imposing disciplinary penalties for employees who are alcoholics and who commit disciplinary offenses.

The arbitrator also found that the grievant had failed to meet a condition of the policy: that the affected employee be enrolled in a rehabilitation program controlled by or approved by the company medical department at the time that the disciplinary offense was committed.

> As the company's policy with regard to help and consideration accorded an employee who is an alcoholic or who suffers from a drinking problem comes into play only when and after the employee qualifies for the "umbrella" protection, I cannot find that the company violated its policy by disciplining the grievant for an offense which took place before his rehabilitative effort, and before the effective point of that policy.[9]

Since the company had the right to impose the penalty of discharge, the arbitrator found, it also had the right to convert it to a lesser penalty, a 21-month suspension.

Here the company's obligation to be of help was subordinated to its contractual right to impose discipline for just cause even when alcoholism was raised as an argument in defense of the grievant. The employer's policy statement was construed as an offer to take alcoholism into account but not as binding commitment because it was not incorporated in the contract. Moreover, the arbitrator, interpreting the policy narrowly, found that it protected only those who had already come forward and sought its "umbrella" of protection. This interpretation followed the argument of the company that its policy is "more of a screen than a shield. The medical department screens discipline only for those employees whose illness it has been able to verify and whose progress in rehabilitation it has been able to track."[10]

Whereas in the first case the arbitrator held that an employee could qualify for protection after committing dischargeable offenses, in the second the arbitrator ruled that the employee must already have admitted his problem to the company medical department and come under the aegis of a rehabilitation program before the offense took place.

Implications of Pre-Registration

In practice a "pre-registration" requirement would probably severely limit an employee's ability to benefit from a company policy favoring rehabilitation, since, as mentioned earlier, "denial" might prevent the alcoholic from seeking help before he was in serious jeopardy. Also, some employees may be reluctant to reveal their problems to their employer, even though they may be willing to take them to an outside treatment source. On the other hand, if an employee does make it known to the employer that he has suffered from alcoholism, the employer may incur the obligation discussed above to try treatment before discipline. For example, a 28-year employee was demoted from his position of principal account clerk for a record of poor performance and attendance extending over a year. An arbitrator ruled that the employer, who maintained an EAP, failed not only to properly warn the grievant that his work was unsatisfactory but also to act upon his history of alcoholism. She noted that a few years before the incidents for which the grievant was demoted he took several weeks of sick leave for treatment of alcoholism. His immediate supervisor as well as the finance officer . . . were aware of [the grievant's] drinking problem. The problem was openly discussed upon grievant's return to work following his treatment.

. . .

. . . While not excusing grievant from direct responsibility, on the basis of their knowledge his supervisors should have been exercising more direct oversight of grievant's work, in which event the problem with the accounts would likely have been discovered [earlier].

. . .

. . . [The grievant's] supervisors knew the [EAP] was available, but they [neither] orally nor in writing counselled grievant to seek assistance there or elsewhere.[11]

The arbitrator directed that the grievant be retained in his original position "but only on the condition that he faithfully and satisfactorily participate in the Employee Assistance Program."

Another arbitrator reinstated an alcoholic employee with the recommendation

> that the grievant's supervisor have a frank discussion with the grievant so that the grievant is made fully aware of the fact that continued poor job performance will not be tolerated unless the grievant agrees to participate in the company's alcohol (and drug) program, cooperating with it in referrals for diagnosis and prescribed therapy. Hopefully, the grievant could then develop into a satisfactory employee, particularly since the company feels that he is honest and hardworking.[12]

Such a recommendation should not be construed to mean that poor job performance becomes acceptable so long as an employee is participating in an EAP. Most EAPs emphasize that participants are expected to meet normal job requirements while they are receiving assistance.

The Uncooperative Employee

In promulgating a policy on alcoholism, a company will often leave itself an escape hatch by providing for dismissal should an alcoholic employee refuse to cooperate or prove unsuccessful at rehabilitation. In one case a telephone company had distributed a "Supervisor's Guide for Dealing With Alcoholism," which recognized alcoholism as an illness and urged that every reasonable effort be directed toward rehabilitating employees. But it also provided for termination "through resignation, dismissal or service pension" for those who were resistant to rehabilitation. The guide summed up policies that had been in effect informally for some time.

Around the time the policy was being formalized, a phone company lineman with nearly 25 years of seniority was discharged for absenteeism caused by drinking and for coming to work on several occasions under the influence of alcohol. His problems with alcohol had become evident on the job about two years before, when he was discharged for driving a company vehicle after having several beers at lunch. He had later been voluntarily reinstated by the company.

A grievance filed on the lineman's behalf over the second discharge contended that, since he was "an admitted alcoholic," the discharge was improper because the company was obliged to help the grievant overcome the illness. The company argued that it had met its obligation inasmuch as supervisors repeatedly had urged the grievant to seek treatment. On several occasions, the company said, he had taken the advice, even enrolling in residential treatment programs, but then had failed to act upon the recommendations of the treatment staff. For example, a recommendation that he join Alcoholics Anonymous was never followed up. The arbitrator concluded that the grievant's supervisors "did exercise a considerable amount of patience in their approach to . . . his problem," given that "their primary responsibility was to see that the work of the department is done." He wrote:

> [T]here was no contractual obligation on the part of the company to do anything more than was done or even to do what it did.
>
> . . .
>
> Furthermore, the conduct of [the grievant], his unwillingness to fully recognize and admit his problem, his failure to follow and adhere to programs and tools recommended to him from professional sources, his lack of effort on his own behalf while aware of what the consequences would be, all leave no basis for concluding that anything more the company might have undertaken to help would have produced a different result.
>
> The greatest responsibility was that of [the grievant] himself, and he did not assume it. He had professional counseling services, particularly at [a residential facility]. Judged by the use he

made of that service, there does not seem to be any reasonable basis for concluding that if the company had also provided counseling service, the result would have been different.

. . .

. . . In short, he did not demonstrate to the satisfaction of the board of arbitration that he intended to do what was necessary in an attempt to overcome his problem.[13]

The discharge was upheld, a result which evidently springs from the proposition that an employer's obligation to help is limited by the willingness of the employee to accept help.

Retaliation Claims

There may be situations in which an employee contends that disciplinary action is being taken against him for refusing to take advantage of an EAP when it is offered to him by the employer. Such was the complaint of a social worker with an admittedly chronic drinking problem who had twice been involved in automobile accidents related to alcohol and had twice had his license suspended. The second suspension had been for two months. During those license suspensions, the employer had also suspended the social worker from employment on the ground that a license was necessary to carry out his duties, which included home visits. The grievant claimed that the suspensions violated the collective bargaining agreement, and he sought back pay for the time lost. Among his arguments was the claim that, in suspending him, the employer was retaliating for his refusal to participate in the state's EAP when he had been advised to do so by supervisors several years before the license suspensions had occurred.

The arbitrator wrote:

I wholeheartedly concur with the union's contention that the state may not retaliate against employees for refusal to participate in the Employee Assistance Program. To allow such retaliation would render the voluntary nature of the program illusory.

While the grievant argues the department retaliated against him for refusal to participate in the EAP, this is not the case. The record is clear that *but for* the loss of license, no action would have been taken.

The critical inquiry is whether the license was necessary to do the job.

The credible evidence establishes that his ability to drive was an essential ingredient of his job duties.

The arbitrator, moreover, found no merit in the grievant's contention that the department could have placed him temporarily in a position which did not require a driver's license. He said:

> The department has repeatedly urged grievant to seek professional help. Grievant has steadfastly refused. He had every right to do so. However, he must be willing to shoulder the burden of consequences for his actions. This is something he is still unwilling to do. Instead, he seeks imposition of a requirement that the department change its methods of operation to accomodate a situation over which it had no control and for which grievant must bear complete and total responsibility. If grievant is not willing to help himself, it is unreasonable to expect others to do so.
>
> . . . There is nothing in the collective bargaining agreement that imposes an affirmative duty on the state to alter its methods of operations, the manner in which services are delivered, or the way in which cases are assigned, in order to address grievant's drinking problem.[14]

Equal Treatment of the Alcoholic Employee

Not only the extent but the selectivity of the employer's obligation to help may be at issue in arbitration cases. An employer policy statement recognizing alcoholism as an illness may leave unclear the exact conditions under which an employee will be offered an opportunity for rehabilitation. As a result, an offer of such an opportunity extended to other alcoholic employees in the past may be cited as a precedent or claimed as an established employer practice by a grievant who is discharged without benefit of a similar offer.

That was the issue in a case of a meter reader who was discharged following a drinking bout for failure to perform his duties. His record for the previous three years—most of his time with the company—had been marred by warnings and suspensions for inadequate performance.

The union argued that the company had erred by regarding the grievant as incompetent rather than recognizing him as a victim of alcoholism, as required by the company's "Drinking and Drug Rehabilitation Program." It asked that he be given an opportunity to demonstrate that his alcoholism was under control, as the company had in the case of two other employees, W. and M. The company had agreed to review their discharges in six months to give the employees an opportunity to demonstrate a record of sobriety and acceptable behavior.

The company objected that W. and M. deserved such an opportunity but that the grievant did not: they had had more seniority and good work records. The grievant had a history of disciplinary infractions. The arbitrator found that

> [t]his distinction is not sufficiently convincing. [The grievant] worked more than 3½ years with the company. And while [the grievant's] work record was not model, there was not sufficient evidence that the other two employees' work records were model ones.
>
> . . . [T]here is no loss to the company if it applies to [the grievant] the same policy it applied to W. and M.

Of course, treating the grievant as an alcoholic would make sense only if he were an alcoholic, but the company was not convinced that he was. It had called attention to the following caution in its alcohol policy statement:

> Nothing in this statement of policy is to be interpreted as constituting a waiver of management's responsibility to maintain discipline or the right to take disciplinary measures, within the framework of the collective bargaining agreement, in the case of unsatisfactory performance or misconduct. The use of alcohol or other substances is not an excuse.

Noting that the grievant had rejected an offer of participation in the company rehabilitation program the previous year, the company said it had concluded that alcohol was not the whole reason for the grievant's failure to work properly. The arbitrator, however, found it "difficult to see how or why [the grievant's] drinking problem was not recognized as serious." He wrote:

> The company maintains that its decision to discharge the grievant was based on his failure to perform his work, and that alcoholism cannot be used as an excuse not to perform one's work. But the company's rehabilitation program becomes an empty gesture if the company refuses to consider that the quality of work performed by an employee may be affected by his alcoholism. Drinking may be the *reason*, and not an *excuse*, for an employee's failure to perform work.[15]

Evaluating Recovery Prospects

In several of the cases discussed in this chapter, the threshold issue was whether the employee was indeed an alcoholic, entitling him to a treatment option in place of discharge. In some instances, however, the critical issue is not whether the employee suffers from alcoholism but whether his chances of recovery are good. The question may be framed as follows: is the employee's prognosis for recovery sufficiently promising to find that the discharge was without just cause?

That question was presented in a case involving a supervisor of five employees in the headquarters of a state corrections department. After lunch one afternoon, the supervisor returned intoxicated to the office, where he became disorderly, disruptive and abusive to coworkers. As a result of this incident, the employer notified him that it believed he no longer had the "credibility" to function as a supervisor, and it demoted him to his previous position of corrections officer.

The union contended that the employee's bizarre behavior resulted from alcoholism, and it argued that the proper course of action was not to discipline him but to offer him a chance for rehabilitation. It noted that just after the incident—and before his demotion—he had enrolled in the state's Employee Assistance Program. The union called attention to the program's policy statement that "[b]ehavioral/medical problems such as alcoholism [and] drug abuse . . . are illnesses or situations that are treatable and/or can be resolved with professional assistance."

The arbitrator ruled that in order to have the discipline sustained, the employer had to show that "it was improbable the grievant would ever be able to fulfill the duties of supervisor." In deciding that issue, the arbitrator relied on the testimony of an expert medical witness, a physician. The witness, who had not examined the grievant, testified that alcoholics can be successfully treated through counseling and support, although many fail in treatment, and said that the recidivism rate is higher for "intermittent" than for chronic alcoholics because of the former group's tendency to fall away from the "support system."

The arbitrator concluded:

> In view of this expert testimony and the grievant's demeanor . . . at the hearing, the arbitrator was impressed and persuaded to believe the grievant could maintain control of his alcoholism problem as long as he continued to participate in the [EAP] . . . and kept his appointments with his therapist. The arbitrator is of the opinion the grievant has the will and motivation to be one of the small percentage of alcoholics who can maintain con-

> trol of his alcoholism . . . . The arbitrator concludes, therefore, it is probable the grievant will be able to fulfill his employment obligations in the future.[16]

The award stated that the decision to demote the grievant without establishing conditions for reinstatement to his supervisory position was not supported by just cause, and the remedy ordered was immediate reinstatement to the original position, but without back pay.

Use of Experts

The foregoing is an example of a case which hinges upon the arbitrator's personal impressions of the grievant's amenability to treatment. Many arbitrators, obviously, may be loathe to take upon themselves the responsibility for judging the grievant's recovery prospects. It is a task more in keeping with the therapeutic than the arbitral function, and it may leave the arbitrator open to manipulation. One way to avoid making the arbitrator the clinical assessor is to introduce as expert evidence the assessments of physicians or other treatment specialists, opinions based on their personal knowledge of the employee. Sometimes the opinions of Alcoholics Anonymous members have been accepted in evidence.[17] Even then, the prognosis is unlikely to be ironclad, since the most experienced therapists usually disclaim any ability to forecast with precision the recovery prospects of a given individual. But at least in such cases the arbitrator's decision is grounded on the record rather than on a layman's intuition.

Another source of testimony on recovery prospects is the staff of the EAP and the counselors or medical consultants who have firsthand knowledge of the employee's progress. However, EAP personnel are usually reluctant to testify, as a matter of policy, for fear of compromising employees' trust in the confidentiality of the program. Employees are hardly likely to take their personal problems to the company EAP if they believe that what they say to counselors may ultimately become part of a disciplinary proceeding. On occasion, EAP personnel will testify but limit their remarks to a statement of whether or not the employee has been participating in the program. Some will testify more fully about the employee's progress, if the employee so requests and consents to release of his records. A sensible practice is for the employer and union to agree in advance on the proper scope of an EAP counselor's participation in an arbitration hearing.

Factors to Consider

What factors are properly taken into account in judging the grievant's prospects for successful rehabilitation? Motivation is clearly a major determinant, at least insofar as it persuades arbitrators. In some of the cases discussed above, the grievant took the initiative in seeking treatment immediately after the incident which precipitated the discharge. Such actions are often interpreted as evidence of motivation to improve, although they can be self-serving: applying to the EAP may be a stratagem to impress the employer and the arbitrator. The critical factor is whether the employee follows through by diligently attending sessions in recommended programs and by making an effort to alter his behavior (see "Post-Discharge Behavior" in Chapter 1).

Summary

In sum, it would seem that the existence of an EAP may give rise to claims that an employee either was not offered a chance for rehabilitation or was discriminated against for refusing such an offer, it being asserted in either case that the employer violated the collective bargaining agreement. Obviously, the decision of an arbitrator in such cases hinges very much upon the particular facts; in each instance, arbitrators must decide whether the normal standards against which disciplinary actions are measured should be altered to take account of the special situation that may have been created when the employer implemented an EAP. To whom and under what circumstances opportunities for assistance are offered become issues subject to scrutiny, because they may be relevant to whether the discipline is supported by just cause. Actions which are arbitrary, capricious, discriminatory, unreasonable or based upon animus certainly cannot be allowed to stand. At the same time, those charged with the responsibility for treating individuals need to be allowed flexibility in order to tailor the treatment to their widely varying needs.

The Rehabilitated Employee

A related issue is the length of time which the employee is to be granted for rehabilitation. If an employer offers an employee rehabilitation leave or agrees to reconsider a discharge after seeing evidence of recovery, must it offer a "reasonable" period of time before requiring the employee to report back to work?

"Reasonable" tends to be undefinable *a priori* because most sophisticated treatment programs are open-ended. In many industries, when an EAP refers an employee to an outside treatment resource, such as a residential program, the typical stay is about 28 days. But the follow-up, involving meetings and counseling sessions, continues for an indefinite period afterward. Determining the point in the treatment at which the employee can be declared ready to resume work is often difficult; expecting an employee to return after a predetermined period with the certificate of a doctor or counselor that he has been "cured" is unrealistic.

The Boston Gas Program

The "six-month program" of the Boston Gas Company, which was involved in the case discussed under "Equal Treatment of the Alcoholic Employee" earlier in this chapter, does set a time for review, evidently with some success. When an employee is discharged for reasons relating to alcoholism, the discharge notice sets a fixed date, about six months later, on which the decision will be reviewed. The notice lays out the steps which must be taken by the employee to secure a favorable review:

> Between now and ____, it is your personal responsibility to take positive action insuring your rehabilitation. You must demonstrate and establish a record of sobriety and acceptable behavior during this period. The services of . . . [the] rehabilitation counselor . . . are available to you. During this period, you must maintain contact with [him] on a monthly basis.
>
> Provided you meet these conditions and provide positive proof of rehabilitation, the company will arrange to evaluate your condition and eligibility for re-employment.
>
> Factors to be considered would include, but are not limited to:

a. Active involvement and attendance in a bona fide rehabilitation program. Documentation of participation and progress to be submitted monthly.
b. A demonstrated record of sobriety and responsibility as evidenced by a clean police record, recommendations from recognized persons or organizations involved in rehabilitation; i.e., Alcoholics Anonymous, Boston Gas rehabilitation counselor, clergy, physicians, etc.
c. A record of gainful employment.
d. A satisfactory physical examination.

It is understood this is *not* a guarantee of re-employment, but an offer to give you re-employment consideration.

By the end of 1981, the six-month program had been offered to six employees. At that time four of the six had met the reinstatement conditions, were re-employed and were satisfactorily performing their duties.[18]

The Boston Gas program is characterized by flexibility at two important points. First, it does not guarantee the employee's return; it merely promises that the discharge will be looked at again. Second, it does not demand that the employee be "cured." It simply asks for "progress" and a convincing demonstration of sobriety and ability to work during the interval between the discharge and the review. The program thus enables each alcoholic employee to be scrutinized individually, and it realistically emphasizes signs of improvement rather than dubious assurances of total recovery.

Rehire Obligations

What do arbitrators generally view as the obligation of an employer to rehire an employee who has undergone or is undergoing treatment in a rehabilitation program? The issue is sometimes raised when there is a difference of opinion between the company and the union about whether the employee has made sufficient progress to warrant reinstatement.

In a steel industry case, the grievant had undergone a six-week course of treatment at a reputable medical institution. A 25-year employee, he had earlier been discharged by the company for tardiness and absences related to alcoholism. The union had filed a grievance against the discharge but withdrew it when the company agreed to consider the grievant a candidate for rehabilitation.

The union argued that the company was obligated to rehire the grievant, on the ground that he had successfully completed the treatment program. It cited the report of program officials, who said that the grievant had made "tremendous progress" and urged his reinstatement. The company, which doubted that the grievant was rehabilitated, maintained that its own medical staff's prognosis for the grievant was not as positive as that of the treatment program staff.

The arbitrator ordered the grievant rehired with back pay. He found that the company gave insufficient weight to the evidence pointing to the grievant's rehabilitation.

> The reports of the company's medical department are not in evidence and no doctor was called to testify as to why the company should accept and act upon the doubts of its in-house physicians rather than the report from the [treatment] program.[19]

The arbitrator also found unpersuasive the company's contention that it had discharged the grievant for an unsatisfactory work record unrelated to alcoholism in addition to the alcohol-related misconduct. The problems with the grievant's work cited by the company, the arbitrator said, "could well be ascribable to alcoholism." (See further discussion of steel industry contractual provisions on alcoholism under "Interpreting a Rehabilitation Clause" in Chapter 8.)

In a related case, the grievant, a bus driver, had been discharged after morphine and other substances were found in a urinalysis. Tests conducted subsequently by his own doctor showed no drugs, and the doctor recommended him for re-employment. The grievant sought an assignment to another job while he rehabilitated himself from the use of drugs.

The arbitrator found "no basis in the contract on which I can order the [employer] to assume the responsibility of rehabilitating persons who have a drug problem." But he noted that the employer had said that it would consider re-employing the grievant after he had been rehabilitated:

> The question arises as to how long the rehabilitation should take before he is given another opportunity . . . .
>
> I make no judgment at this time as to when . . . the [employer] might review whether [the grievant] should be reinstated. This is a new area in our experience, and I have no basis for setting any particular time limits. I do believe nevertheless that the [employer] should undertake to review the matter within a reasonable period of time in view of the evidence submitted by [the grievant's] own physician.[20]

4

Standards of Proof and Investigative Evidence

Quantum of Proof in Alcohol and Drug Cases

A perennial issue in discharge cases is the quantum of proof required to establish just cause and support the discipline imposed—whether it should be a "preponderance of the evidence," "clear and convincing evidence," "evidence sufficient to convince a reasonable mind of guilt" or proof "beyond a reasonable doubt." Some arbitrators believe that exceptionally high standards should apply in cases "where the alleged offense involves an element of moral turpitude or criminal intent."[1] Underpinning this belief is the notion that upholding the discipline would lastingly stigmatize the employee. Professor Benjamin Aaron has explained this rationale as follows:

> Since upholding disciplinary penalties for [alleged criminal offenses] or similar acts permanently brands an employee just as surely as a criminal conviction would, the arbitrator will generally insist . . . that the employer prove his charges beyond a reasonable doubt.[2]

Another version of the stigma theory has been put forward by Arbitrator Russell A. Smith:

> [A]lleged misconduct of a kind which carries the stigma of general social disapproval as well as disapproval under accepted canons of plant discipline should be clearly and convincingly established by the evidence. Reasonable doubts raised by the proofs should be resolved in favor of the accused. This may mean that the employer will at times be required, for want of sufficient proof, to withhold or rescind disciplinary action which in fact is

fully deserved, but this kind of result is inherent in any civilized system of justice.[3]

On the other hand, one sees the contention by Arbitrator W. Willard Wirtz that "the technicalities of criminal law are a poor guide to labor relations,"[4] and even Professor Aaron has called attention to the fact that the criminal law analogy may be abused:

> Those who are prone indiscriminately to apply the criminal law analogy in the arbitration of all discharge cases overlook the fact that the employer and employee do not stand in the relationship of prosecutor and defendant . . . . At stake is not only the matter of justice to an individual employee, important as that principle is, but also the preservation and development of the collective bargaining relationship.[5]

The Question of Stringency

The relevant question here is the stringency of the standard of proof that is required in alcohol and drug cases. Some drug cases—those involving trafficking in controlled substances, for example—no doubt might be said to entail criminal intent. In one case, a grievant who was alleged to have sold pills to fellow employees was reinstated by an arbitrator, who applied a relatively strict standard:

> However [the] various standards of proof are described, arbitrators do apply a more stringent standard in cases involving moral turpitude or criminal conduct. In this case, the arbitrator will apply the more stringent standard; he must be completely convinced that [the grievant] engaged in the conduct alleged.

After reviewing the evidence, the arbitrator concluded that the grievant had admitted selling the pills but that there was no direct evidence on a crucial point—whether the grievant had offered them for sale as a controlled substance (which they were not):

> Absent corroborative evidence, the arbitrator is unwilling to draw the inference that [the grievant] held out to purchasers that the pills were a controlled substance. This conclusion is compelled by the more stringent standard of proof applied to the allegations of criminal conduct in this case.[6]

In another case, involving a grievant arrested for allegedly possessing heroin, the arbitrator ruled:

> [The] standard is whether or not the credible evidence raises a reasonable doubt as to the knowing possession of narcotics by the grievant.[7]

Other arbitrators, while holding to the stigma theory, have not seen the need in drug cases to impose a burden of proof greater than "preponderance of the evidence":

> The union's position is, and I agree, that the company must establish by a preponderance of the evidence (as distinguished from the criminal test of proof beyond a reasonable doubt) that the grievants were guilty of possession or use of marijuana. . . .
>
> The loss of a job may very well have more serious consequences to the life of an employee and the lives of his family than a conviction and a jail sentence. Particularly is this true when a discharge is sustained based on the charge of possession or use of drugs. Accordingly, a close analysis of the evidence is required.[8]

Is the Stigma Theory Appropriate?

The stigma theory assumes that a stigma arises from a finding of "criminal intent."[9] In the case of prescription drug abuse the theory is inapposite, however, because the conduct may be intensely stigmatizing—perhaps seriously diminishing the chances of obtaining other employment—without being illegal. If stigma alone were the criterion, the beyond-a-reasonable-doubt standard might be invoked in situations not remotely related to criminal behavior—surely a disproportionate response.

It should be borne in mind that the employer–employee relationship, as Professor Aaron has noted, is fraught with considerations quite different from those of a criminal justice system. Among them is the practical necessity of maintaining the safety and productivity of the workplace. Viewed in this light, the issue is not whether there is enough evidence to punish an individual but whether there is a reasonable basis for taking preventive or protective measures to maintain safety and productivity when these are threatened by drugs.

Moreover, where the parties themselves have expressed a preference for the standard to be used, they have at times opted for a lesser burden of proof. A public employer and its employees, in one drug case, had agreed to a contract provision that the "burden of proof, even in serious matters which might constitute a crime, shall be preponderance of the evidence on the record and shall in no case be proof beyond a reasonable doubt."[10]

In any event, in disciplinary arbitrations, including those involving alcohol and drugs, what is generally at issue is not employee "fault" or "innocence" but whether the employer had "just cause." The ultimate criterion remains: is the arbitrator, who is presumed to be a rational and fair-minded decision-maker, convinced that just cause existed under all the facts and circumstances? If applied consistently, there is no reason why that criterion should be insufficient to protect the grievant, regardless of the odiousness of the alleged offense.

The Grievant as "Addict"

Attaching the status of "addict" to an employee can have consequences leading to discharge or to an offer of rehabilitation, but in either case the question is likely to turn upon an assessment of the grievant. How well-grounded must that assessment be? In one case, a 16-year employee of a tool company was discharged after pleading guilty to a criminal charge of attempting to obtain cocaine by means of a fraudulent doctor's prescription. The arbitrator noted that there was a company rule against "reporting for work under the influence of alcohol or drugs." The grievant had not infringed the rule, but he was the subject of a report by a physician who examined him at the request of county authorities after his arrest. The doctor found that the grievant's account of his past use of cocaine "makes for the unquestionable conclusion that he was addicted to this drug." The arbitrator ruled that the "evidence tended to prove that [the grievant] was a narcotic addict." He wrote:

> Cocaine is a well-known stimulant-type narcotic drug derived from the coca plant which is native to South America. . . . In advanced stages, cocaine addicts are dangerous and may attack friends or innocent by-standers. The potential industrial hazards of having a cocaine addict as a fellow worker were clearly defined by the testimony of [Dr. M., another physician who provided evidence].
>
> . . .
>
> Drug addiction not only depraves the victim but it, rightly, carries a social stigma. The fact that addiction had not yet reached the stage where it directly affected [the grievant's] ability to properly perform his duties is not determinative.[11]

The discharge was upheld by a majority formed by the arbitrator and the employer-appointed member of the three-person panel, but the union-appointed member wrote a dissent which focused on the gross disparity between the theoretical description of the addict and the grievant's actual performance on the job:

> Testimony by [Dr. M] pertinent to usage of cocaine in the amounts inferred by the company and over the period indicated by the prosecution . . . would have clearly shown a deleterious effect upon the user. Yet [the grievant] on the eighth day after examination by [the county-appointed physician] did not exhibit any of the symptoms described by [Dr. M] and attributable to an addict.
>
> . . .
>
> . . . [The grievant's] record of employment was, admittedly, excellent. His behavior and compatibility with his fellow employees was beyond reproach, yet he now stands convicted in the eyes of the community [as] a "drug addict," not by action of the court, but of the company.[12]

The outcome of this case was probably more stigmatizing to the grievant than the outcome of the criminal justice proceeding stemming from the same incident. Yet no exceptionally high standard of proof was imposed. On the contrary, once the label of "addict" was attached to the grievant, a number of supposed traits of addicts were associated with the grievant by inference, even though his work record provided no basis for concern about his conduct.

Diagnostic Criteria

A more sophisticated approach to the same question would make use of the standard diagnostic criteria for "substance use disorders" promulgated by the American Psychiatric Association (see "Drug Abuse as a Treatable Disorder" in Chapter 2). Under these criteria, a disorder is divided into two components: "substance abuse" and "substance dependence." An individual may exhibit one or both components. Substance abuse is established by such indicators as long-term use, repeated intoxication, and impairment of social and occupational functioning. Substance dependence is present if the individual develops a "tolerance" for the substance, requiring greater and greater doses to achieve the same effect, and suffers "withdrawal" effects when usage stops.

Applying these criteria to the facts of the cocaine case discussed above, it becomes immediately apparent that the grievant did not exhibit one of the substance abuse indicators in that cocaine had not impaired his occupational functioning; his work record was flawless. Moreover, substance dependence is not associated with cocaine in the APA diagnostic schema because physiological dependence has not been established.

Evidence From Searches

Arbitrators in alcohol and drug cases generally recognize, at least to some degree, an employee's right to be free of intrusive searches by employers. As one arbitrator has commented:

> Employees must be accorded their right of privacy and there is no absolute right of an employer to search personal effects.[13]

Some arbitrators have even maintained that employers have no authority to search unless accorded that authority in the contract. Nevertheless, the doctrine of employee privacy frequently has given way to a countervailing principle: the legitimate need of the employer to investigate fully allegations of breaches of the rules. Many arbitrators have affirmed an employer's authority to invade an employee's privacy by searching his person, personal possessions or locker for contraband substances when an infraction of plant rules is reported.

Even in the case quoted above, the arbitrator agreed that an employee deserved a suspension for refusing to permit a search, although he held that discharge was too severe. The employee, one of two grievants accused of drinking alcoholic beverages in the women's room, had rebuffed the employer's attempt to have her open her purse to see if it contained a liquor bottle. The union argued that the employer had no authority to inspect the contents of employees' purses. But the arbitrator held that her refusal amounted to insubordination inasmuch as

> Having received such a complaint and regardless of its accuracy, the company was obligated to investigate and . . . could request an explanation.

The employer-appointed arbitrator concurred in the reinstatement but dissented from the award of back pay beyond the suspension period:

> The [grievant's] failure to co-operate in the company's enquiry as to their unusual actions cannot be condoned nor result in a monetary penalty to the company.[14]

Probable Cause

Some arbitrators have held that at least in those situations in which a police officer would have authority to search a suspect—that is, where the supervisor has "probable cause" to believe an "industrial felony" has been committed—the searching of an employee for alcohol or drugs is justified. An arbitrator upheld a 15-day suspension of a grievant for refusing to reveal whether he was hiding a bottle of liquor. A supervisor testified that he had seen the grievant drink from the bottle, had watched him hastily stuff the bottle under his sweater and had smelled alcohol on his breath. When confronted later by the supervisor and other managers, the grievant refused an order to unbutton the sweater. Protesting the suspension, the union argued that "the federal and state constitutions protect individuals in their right of personal privacy and such searches are not a condition of employment." The arbitrator held:

> In criminal cases, an officer who has probable cause to believe a felony has been committed and probable cause to believe that a specific individual committed such a felony may arrest the individual and search him in connection with the arrest. There is *no* constitutional protection against such a search.
>
> It is quite inappropriate to attempt to establish an exact parallel between rights of citizens on the street and employees in the plant. When employees take an employment, they do so subject to normal restrictions inherent in a crowded industrial setting. The right of management to fairly operate its business without undue impediment must be balanced against the right of the employees to continue to enjoy their civil rights to the fullest. However the two will clash and in the factual setting of this case, it is not inappropriate to treat a supervisor by analogy to a peace officer. . . .
>
> In this situation [the supervisor's] observations of grievant and detection of alcohol on his breath, are entirely credible. . . . Therefore [the supervisor] had probable cause to believe that a serious plant rule violation (here use of alcoholic beverage can be viewed as the equivalent of an industrial felony) was being committed. . . . [A]n order to grievant to unbutton his sweater . . . was entirely supportable and within management's prerogative to maintain plant discipline.[15]

Constitutional Rights and the Workplace

In a similar case, a supervisor had spotted an employee removing a tobacco-like substance from a small container and suspected that the substance was a drug. The employee placed the substance in his pocket and refused to remove it for inspection, as requested by the supervisor. He was discharged. In upholding the discharge the arbitrator commented:

> The union argues with conviction that the employer has attempted in this case to place the burden on the employee of proving his innocence, and that this is contrary to the traditions of our society. Of course, in criminal proceedings the burden is on the state to prove guilt beyond a reasonable doubt, and the accused is entitled to a presumption of innocence. But the limitations imposed upon the state with respect to criminal punishment are not applicable in any wholesale manner to disciplinary action taken by an employer. The Fourth and Fourteenth Amendments do prevent a state from conducting unreasonable searches and seizures, but this prohibition would not have direct application to a private employer's demand that an employee give an explanation of suspicious conduct occurring during working hours and on company property. . . . Moreover, the facts . . . suggest that if [the supervisor] were a police officer he would have been entitled to search [the grievant] without a warrant. Constitutional protections therefore do not shelter [the grievant] from appropriate employer discipline. . . .
>
> In any event, this is not a case in which the employer has placed the original burden of proving innocence upon an accused employee. This is instead a case in which the events observed by [a supervisor] established a *prima facie* case that the employee had engaged in conduct which justified discipline. In such a case it is appropriate to place the burden upon the employee to rebut the *prima facie* case by giving an explanation of his conduct and demonstrating the fallacy or at least a weakness in the *prima facie* case. [The grievant] refused to do this, and the *prima facie* case remained against him.[16]

An arbitrator also found no constitutional bar to drug searches in a case involving a supermarket employee upon whom security agents found amphetamines. The union argued that the pills should be excluded as evidence because they were the fruits of a search that violated the employee's Fourth Amendment rights. The union argued that the circumstances of the search—the employee was handcuffed—strongly suggested that he had not consented to it. The arbitrator wrote:

> [T]he constitutional protection against unreasonable searches and seizures does not apply against a private company to prevent their searching an employee at his place of employment, under suspicious circumstances. . . . Arbitrators are concerned with the rights of privacy of employees, but if there is reasonable protection of this right, evidence procured as a result of search, even without permission of the employee, has been admitted and considered by arbitrators in determining the guilt of employees.[17]

Evidence secured during a police search for drugs has been held admissible in arbitration even though the evidence was considered inadmissible in a criminal prosecution. For instance, marijuana that was declared inadmissible as criminal evidence against a flight attendant was admitted in evidence in an arbitration hearing stemming from the same incident. The grievant had been arrested as she deplaned, and a search of her luggage uncovered the marijuana. She was accused of drug possession, but the charges were subsequently dropped because the search was considered to be constitutionally defective. The airline nevertheless discharged the grievant for possessing drugs on company premises and while in uniform. The arbitrator reviewed the argument against the admissibility of the main evidence:

> The union contends that the search of grievant was in violation of her rights against unreasonable searches and seizures guaranteed by the Fourth Amendment to the U.S. Constitution. It argues that the search was illegal and that the evidence obtained as a result of the search was inadmissible and should not be considered by the [arbitration] board. It says that absent the fruits of the search the company has produced no evidence that the grievant was guilty of possessing an illegal drug and that the company had no grounds for discharging grievant.
>
> . . .
>
> I find the . . . argument to be without merit. The Supreme Court of the United States has long held that evidence obtained in violation of the unreasonable search and seizure provisions of the Fourth Amendment to the Federal Constitution is inadmissible in criminal cases. In 1961 the Court held that this exclusionary rule was applicable to criminal proceedings in state courts. *Mapp v. Ohio,* 367 U.S. 643. But there is no definitive ruling of the court making this rule applicable in civil proceedings. And the United States Court of Appeals for the Fifth Circuit has said "as this is not a criminal prosecution but merely an effort to effect a forfeiture arising from illegal use of the property involved, the legality of the search and seizure cannot be raised." *Martin v. United States,* 277 F.2d 785, 786 (1960) . . . .

> . . . I . . . hold that the evidence obtained by the officers in this case as a result of the search of the grievant's possessions was admissible.[18]

Personal Property Searches

While many searches are carried out on the employer's property, so that the employee may have relatively narrow grounds for objecting, at times the employer will attempt to search personal property, such as an employee's car. May an employee's refusal to permit a search be taken as evidence of guilt? In one instance, the grievant had been named by another employee as a seller of marijuana:

> [T]he company attempted [to obtain] additional corroboration of [the accuser's] story by requesting [the grievant] to open his car. [The grievant] refused to permit the company to search the interior of the car, but did allow [a supervisor] to inspect the car's trunk, if he wished. The employer contends this refusal constitutes "proof" of [the grievant's] guilt. . . . The arbitrator disagrees. [The grievant's] reluctance to allow a thorough search of his car is circumstantial evidence, at best, to the contention he was selling marijuana. The mere fact that he refused such a search is only "suspicious" behavior, and does not constitute proof sufficient to corroborate the allegations.[19]

When drugs are discovered in a car, resulting in criminal charges against two employee passengers, is it discriminatory to suspend one of the employees but not the other? A car in which two civilian employees of an Air Force base were riding was stopped at the base gate for a routine check. The guards, using drug detection dogs, found marijuana, and, as a result, a criminal charge of possession was lodged against both. One of the employees was given a five-day suspension by the employer. He grieved, arguing, among other things, that he and the other employee "should have been treated alike because they were both charged with the same offense."

The arbitrator ruled as follows:

> In order for the union to apply the concept of unequal or disparate treatment in this case, the union must show that the grievant and [the other employee] received inconsistent discipline for engaging in the same type of misconduct. . . . It is an undisputed fact that marijuana was found on the grievant and not on [the other employee]; so the arbitrator finds no merit in the union's argument that the men should have been treated the same.[20]

In the same decision, the arbitrator upheld the validity of the search, despite the grievant's claim that the officers had gone beyond a legal search for drugs and had conducted an illegal search for weapons as well.

> The arbitrator finds that the weapons search was a reasonable precaution in a case involving illegal possession of narcotics.[21]

The award also explicitly approved the use of dogs and implicitly endorsed the practice of conducting spot checks of employee vehicles.

Testimony of Undercover Agents

The testimony of undercover agents, either police officers or private detectives hired by the employer, is often introduced either directly or indirectly in discipline cases involving drugs. Such testimony presents peculiar evidentiary problems, in part because the agents may use deception in their dealings with other employees or may seek to maintain anonymity while reporting information injurious to the grievant. Arbitrators vary considerably in the weight that they assign to agents' testimony or written reports.

Uncorroborated Evidence

Is the uncorroborated eyewitness testimony of an undercover agent sufficient to find just cause for discharge? In a significant case, the employer introduced the daily written reports of a Pinkerton investigator who, the company said, had observed "shocking, blatant and 'wide-open' incidents of marijuana use in the plant." The agent himself also testified, stating that he had observed the five grievants smoking and exchanging marijuana. The grievants, who had been discharged for violating a rule against possession of marijuana, denied the accusation. The arbitrator noted that no physical evidence of marijuana use had been produced, that the grievants stoutly denied the accusation and that supervisors had testified that they personally knew of no marijuana use in the plant. Overruling the discharge, he wrote:

> When this arbitrator considers the total lack of any corroborating evidence in support of [the agent's] testimony against the emphatic denials of each of the grievants, he is compelled to

> conclude that the evidence of guilt does not meet the "clear and convincing" standard which is appropriate for cases of this kind. Although the testimony of any accused person must be viewed with some skepticism, the testimony of an employee with a good prior record, as is the case with each of the grievants, should be considered very carefully. While, in the opinion of this arbitrator, it is more likely that an accused employee will testify falsely in his own behalf than that an undercover agent will testify falsely against an accused employee, this arbitrator is of the opinion that the testimony of an outside investigator requires some corroboration for clear and convincing proof of guilt in the face of an emphatic denial of guilt by an employee with a prior good employment record.[22]

The same result was reached in a case in which an undercover agent testified to witnessing the use and sale of marijuana in a plant over a period of weeks. His written reports were also introduced, along with a laboratory report identifying a substance he acquired during the investigation as marijuana. The arbitrator reinstated the grievants with back pay, reasoning that

> [t]he undercover agent and his reports cannot be used alone to establish guilt or innocence in a matter of this sort. There must be other evidence to substantiate, corroborate, verify, uphold and establish beyond any reasonable doubt that these individuals were involved in illegal drug activity in and about the facility.
>
> . . . The company just did not have sufficient proof in order to sustain the charges as brought. Just cause has not been established and while the testimony of the undercover agent seemed forthright it must fall if it stands alone.[23]

Credibility of Testimony

In a related case, however, the arbitrator gave more credit to the testimony of the agent, who said that the three grievants had passed marijuana to him. Finding that the grievants "did not testify at all with the 'demeanor' of credible witnesses," the arbitrator upheld their discharges with the following comment:

> [I]f, *with no more appearing,* we were to believe the dischargee's bare denial over the private investigator's bare assertion, we would be "putting out of business," in employee-discharge cases, the members of a wholly respectable vocation who are much-used to find missing persons, to find missing heirs, to gather evidence for both plaintiffs and defendants in civil suits and for defendants in criminal actions. . . . The next step would be to discredit *any* furtive surveillance. And then we might find that we had really disrupted the maintenance of plant discipline

> in just the sort of situations where furtive surveillance is indispensably necessary. The union and the members of the "unit" have an interest equal to that of the employer in the maintenance of plant discipline in just such situations.
>
> . . .
>
> It is true that [the agent] lied to, and otherwise deceived, the grievants in order to "lend color" to his "cover"; but that was a part of his job.[24]

Similarly, an arbitrator upheld a discharge for trafficking in marijuana based solely upon the testimony of an undercover agent whom the arbitrator found to be "a bona fide expert witness in the area of narcotics and controlled substance investigations." The arbitrator remarked:

> [The undercover agent] testifies under oath that he witnessed, on at least six separate occasions, [the grievant] directly participating in use of, or otherwise trafficking in, a controlled substance (marijuana) on company time and/or property. He further denies any possibility of mistaken identity and/or animus against grievant.
>
> . . .
>
> The company obviously bears the burden of proof as to "just cause" discharge. The . . . [task of establishing the agent's] possible dishonesty is, however, an affirmative one in which the burden of proof transfers to union/grievant.[25]

Another arbitrator upheld the discharge of a grievant who was accused of handing a marijuana cigarette to an undercover agent, although he reinstated several other grievants implicated by the same investigator (who testified under the *nom de guerre* of "agent 100"). Each grievant's case was a discrete credibility contest:

> On the one hand we have the [uncorroborated] testimony of agent 100, uncorroborated because testimony by undercover agents seldom can be corroborated. On the other hand, we have the forthright denials of each of the four grievants, supported by strong character-endorsing testimony by the leaderman in the shipping department, a fellow laborer, and the president of the local union.
>
> My credibility resolutions are based upon my observation of each of the witnesses, coupled with whether their testimony, as a whole, held together logically.[26]

Lack of Direct Testimony

At times the undercover agent may not testify. In one case, the grievant had been discharged for selling marijuana to a private investigator hired by the employer. The incident also resulted in criminal charges against the grievant, and, possibly for reasons connected with the criminal proceedings, the agent declined to testify at the arbitration hearing. The company's case consisted of the testimony of the supervisor to whom the agent reported. The arbitrator ruled:

> The testimony . . . was pure hearsay from beginning to end . . . I find the hearsay recital to be an entirely inadequate basis on which to destroy a man's career, job rights and essential livelihood, not to mention the stain upon his reputation and the resulting difficulty of finding another job.
>
> . . .
>
> . . . Upon a record containing not a word of testimony by the agent himself, the employer asks the arbitrator to find that [the grievant's] involvement in the sale of marijuana was sufficiently established, albeit by hearsay evidence, and that his discharge should accordingly be sustained as based on just cause.
>
> . . .
>
> Some kinds of hearsay no doubt are more compelling than others and carry a certain degree of probability. But in all or substantially all cases which the arbitrator can envisage, there must be apart from the hearsay a core of competent, reliable and credible evidence which the hearsay corroborates.
>
> Especially is this standard mandatory where the contested issue is such a serious one as here, on which turn a man's livelihood and reputation. The arbitrator believes it would be unconscionable to uphold [grievant's] discharge solely on a hearsay account by [a supervisor] who does not himself know the actual facts.

In a footnote, the arbitrator added:

> Without [the agent's] testimony we do not know whether, for example, there may have been entrapment; whether he himself may have triggered the episode by acting as an *agent provocateur;* or whether there were other surrounding circumstances bearing upon [the grievant's] involvement, if any, and the degree of his guilt.[27]

5

Medical and Technical Evidence in Alcohol Cases

Lay Observation

Although arbitrators scrutinize carefully the quality and quantity of lay testimony offered to establish that an employee was intoxicated, there is little disagreement that, in principle, the observations of lay witnesses are sufficient to establish intoxication. The witnesses do not necessarily need to be medically qualified, nor does their testimony necessarily need to be supported by blood tests or other medical evaluations. In a case in which an employee was discharged for being drunk, the company relied principally on the testimony of a foreman who said he concluded that the grievant was intoxicated because his breath smelled of alcohol, his clothes seemed disheveled and "he staggered a little" when he walked. The arbitrator upheld the discharge despite the union's objection that no medical tests had been performed:

> [T]he company is correct in its contention that inebriation is a condition which is sufficiently common in everyday experience for a witness, such as the foreman, to be permitted to recount ordinary observations. When so serious and final a sanction as discharge is involved, it is well for as many definite criteria to be cited as possible. However, on this score alone a discharge in this instance could be supported.[1]

Lay observation is a subjective test at best, but the classic symptoms of intoxication are, after all, well-known. They have been catalogued by an arbitrator as follows:

The signs are: speech—thick, slurred, loud; flushed face; general appearance—dishevelment, dirtiness, unkemptness; appearance of eyes—red, watery, heavy lids, fixed pupils; breath—foul, distinctive odor of various intoxicants; gait—walking unsteadily, deliberately and overcarefully, swaying, weaving, stooped; behavior—excessive silliness or boisterousness, etc.[2]

By the same token, the failure of witnesses to observe the critical signs of intoxication can be equally persuasive. In one case, for example, the arbitrator found it

difficult to understand how a member of management could walk [with the allegedly intoxicated grievant] fifty to sixty feet from the work area to his office, talk to the grievant for about fifteen or twenty minutes, . . . ask a supervisor to observe him . . . , walk with him from the office to an automobile, walk from an automobile to the emergency room of the hospital and back to the automobile; upon return to the plant walk back to the office and *never* observe his walk, never [see] him stagger or weave: in fact, he could not even testify how the employee walked.[3]

Testimony or Test Results Alone

On the other hand, many arbitrators have been wary of relying solely on the impressions of witnesses, primarily because of the wide variations in perception that are possible. Looking disheveled or having an unsteady gait can be attributed to reasons other than inebriation, and, without corroboration by tests, there is a danger that innocent symptoms may be mistaken for the effects of alcohol. As one arbitrator cautioned:

There is no question that the company has the right to discipline, suspend, and even to discharge, and to make rules not in conflict with the bargaining agreement. However, it is incumbent upon the company, in making of its rules, to set standards or criteria by which all employees must be judged . . . . The opinions of supervisory personnel as to speech, breath, eyes, or otherwise are, at best, very poor criteria. A blood alcohol test or a urine test all are much better criteria, if an alcohol level is set in advance as the point at which the rule is violated or not violated.[4]

At the same time, running through the case literature is a strong thread of suspicion regarding discharges which rely on blood alcohol test results alone, without corroboration from witnesses who saw the employee in an impaired state. The reasons for not "going by the numbers" of a blood test were trenchantly argued in an award that dealt with an employee who gave little outward appearance of intoxication although his test results showed considerable blood alcohol:

The Physician's Sobriety Report shows that he passed the clinical tests with flying colors. Aside from "odor of alcohol: moderate" and "speech: fair" on a scale running "normal, fair, slurred, stuttering, confused, incoherent, jerky," he got top rating on all items; color of face, apparently normal; clothes, orderly; mental state, polite; unusual actions, none; eyes, normal; pupils, normal; balance, good; walking, sure; turning, sure; finger to nose, sure. His pulse was 116, regular. Yet under Impression on Examination the doctor wrote, "possibly under the influence of alcohol."

. . .

. . . Only the fact that management had sent him in for a sobriety test could have caused the examining physician to write, "Possibly under the influence of alcohol." He certainly did not follow the advice of the British Medical Association and rely solely upon his clinical findings in making his first judgment.[5]

Testimony and Test Results Together

In some cases, the arbitrator found neither the blood test results nor the eye-witness testimony compelling but believed that, taken together, they provided an adequate basis for decision. In one case, for example, the arbitrator wrote:

The laboratory report does not specifically prove that [the grievant] was drunk at the time he gave a sample of blood. BUT, it does prove beyond any reasonable doubt that he had had several drinks of some type of alcoholic beverage on the morning in question—enough to say that if he were a typical non-drinker he would have been "double drunk," as the company contends. [The grievant's blood test registered more than twice the legal intoxication level under the state motoring laws].

. . .

In view of the admissibility of the blood alcohol test which conclusively proved that the grievant was at least *under the influence* of alcohol . . . ; and, in view of the obvious recognition by four members of management that he appeared to be intoxicated, your arbitrator must uphold the company's contention that it had proper and just "cause" to suspend and later discharge the grievant . . . .[6]

Refusal to Take or Offer a Test

More complex is the question of whether an employer may require an employee to take a blood alcohol test or—to put it another way—whether refusal to take a test amounts to just cause for discipline. It has sometimes been argued that requiring an employee to submit to a blood test is a gross invasion of privacy and perhaps of constitutional rights—particularly when the employer is a public agency. This argument has found some support in arbitral opinion. It has been held that there must be evidence from which it can be found that the employee has either expressly or implicitly consented to having his blood drawn; a waiver of constitutional rights cannot be presumed.[7]

Where the collective bargaining agreement provides for a blood test, the provision might be deemed tantamount to a waiver in advance of the employee's right to object, but such provisions are far from universal in labor agreements. Other arbitrators have perceived no fundamental conflict with personal rights. As one arbitrator remarked, "asking an employee to take a blood test is clearly as much for his protection as for the company's."[8]

Blood tests could be viewed as inadmissible because they compel the employee to incriminate himself, but analogies to the criminal justice system, as noted in the previous chapter, can be misleading. In the workplace there is a critical need to preserve a safe and productive environment. The right of the employer to remove an impaired employee is unquestioned, and blood tests may be viewed as one method of ascertaining impairment.

Refusals in the Face of Contract Provisions or Company Policy

Nevertheless, there is support for the view that an employee's refusal to take a blood test does not by itself justify discipline, and there have been decisions invalidating such discipline, even where the collective bargaining agreement or company policy specifically required the tests. In one case, the grievant, a truck driver, had been discharged when he refused to take a blood test following a minor accident at a loading dock. The collective bargaining agreement prohibited working while under the influence of alcohol and authorized the employer to require the employee to submit to a sobriety test "when an employer has good reason to believe that an employee may be under the influence of alcohol." The agreement went on to state that if an employee refused, "this shall be *prima facie* evidence of being under the influence." The arbitrator reasoned as follows:

> This provision clearly does not make refusal to take the sobriety test a punishable offense; the offense to be proven remains drinking or being under the influence of alcohol. The last sentence makes refusal to take the test *prima facie* evidence, not *conclusive* evidence, [of] being under the influence, plainly indicating that the *prima facie* case can be refuted by other evidence.
>
> . . .
>
> In the present case, the presumption that [the grievant] was intoxicated arising from his failure to take the test does not require the union to persuade the arbitrator that [the grievant] was in fact sober. It requires only that there be evidence from which the arbitrator can find that a reasonable person could be persuaded that [the grievant] was sober. . . .
>
> . . .
>
> The evidence . . . raises very serious doubts as to whether [the grievant] was in fact intoxicated. His gait was steady, his eyes were normal, his face was not flushed, and the evidence is not persuasive that his speech was any more incoherent and slurred than normal when he is excited. . . .
>
> . . .
>
> [I]t would take a brash and self-certain arbitrator to declare that no reasonable person could conclude that [the grievant] was sober.[9]

The arbitrator decided that the employer had not proven that the grievant was under the influence of alcohol, and reinstatement was ordered.

In a related case, involving a bus driver for a public authority, the collective bargaining agreement provided that employees would "observe and conform" to rules which included the following:

> Employees suspected of being under the influence of alcohol, narcotics or dangerous drugs shall submit to an examination, including a chemical analysis of samples of blood or urine, by a recognized hospital, clinic or laboratory. Refusal to submit to such examination will be considered an admission of being under the influence of alcohol, narcotics or dangerous drugs.

The grievant refused to take a blood test after the bus he was driving became involved in an accident. He was requested to take the test by a supervisor who testified to having smelled alcohol on the driver's breath. The grievant said he refused to go to the laboratory to which the supervisor directed him because he believed the laboratory to be partial to the company.

The arbitrator found that neither the supervisor "nor any of the other witnesses described or related any objective manifestations of impaired ability." He wrote:

> Frankly, . . . some doubt exists . . . as to who, under the rules, does have the right to determine which hospital, clinic or laboratory should be used. . . . If the rule does not give [the grievant] the right to decide which hospital, clinic or laboratory was to be used, then perhaps it behooves the company, through the bargaining process if necessary, to clarify the exact meaning of that rule in order to avoid the recurrence of this confusion in the future. There does not seem to be, therefore, any hard evidence of bad faith on the part of grievant that he refused per se to submit to a sobriety test.[10]

A similar result was reached in another case involving a transit employee. A garage mechanic who refused to take a blood test was reinstated because the employer had never made known to employees its policy of requiring such tests when employees are suspected of alcoholic impairment; the policy was embodied in a memorandum which circulated only among supervisory personnel. The arbitrator concluded:

> While Article II [of the collective bargaining agreement] confirms the authority's right to promulgate work rules relating to conditions of employment, it provides that such work rules should be published and then sets forth a procedure if "any changes or amendments of existing work rules" are to be promulgated. . . .
>
> . . .
>
> Grievant's discharge was clearly predicated both upon his alleged intoxication and his refusal to submit to a blood test. Without even prior notice of any such requirement to the employees or the union, this unilateral change in working conditions was ineffective. In such circumstances, grievant was under no obligation to comply with the authority's direction.[11]

The Factual Question of Refusal

Even where the contract clearly obligates an employee to submit to a test, the factual question of whether the employee did or did not refuse to submit to a test may become an issue in arbitration. A penalty of discharge was held to be too severe in the case of a transit maintenance worker who declined to sign a test consent form, even though the company rule stated that "refusal [by an employee suspected of alcohol or drug intoxication] to submit immediately to this test will constitute acknowledgement by him of his guilt." The arbitrator found that the grievant was in fact willing to submit to the test (a urinalysis) but balked at signing the consent form proferred by the investigators because his poor reading ability prevented him from understanding the document:

> It . . . appears that the grievant was not offered the urine bottle for the obtaining of his urinalysis until he would sign the consent form. The issue then became one of signing the consent form and not the furnishing of urine.

The arbitrator reduced the discharge to reinstatement with partial back pay since

> [a]t best, the record discloses an employee in an unsafe condition to work and the cause or causes of his condition . . . unknown.[12]

Adverse Inferences

If arbitrators have proven reluctant to uphold penalties for merely refusing a test, they have often been ready to draw an adverse inference from the employee's failure to avail himself of the opportunity to disprove the allegation by taking the test. In the cases of the truck driver and the bus driver, discussed above, the grievants were denied back pay, evidently on the ground that the employee, even if not culpable, had contributed to forcing the case to arbitration by declining a chance to clear himself.

In the bus driver's case the arbitrator reasoned:

> Grievant's refusal, or his conduct which made it appear to [the supervisor] that he was refusing, to take the sobriety test may have been in good faith. That does not necessarily justify his conduct. For that reason, he should bear the loss which his conduct, for whatever reason, caused.[13]

The arbitrator in the truck driver's case concluded:

> The company acted reasonably and did everything it could to persuade [the grievant] to take the test and to take it under circumstances which were acceptable to him. [The grievant's] loss of earnings between the time of his refusal to take the test and the determination that the *prima facie* case was rebutted should not be borne by the company which made every effort to avoid that loss.[14]

In both cases, a discharge was converted into a lengthy disciplinary suspension for an employee whose culpability on the main charge was never established.

Where witnesses have never credibly testified to seeing behavior consistent with a finding of intoxication, a common theory is that an employee's refusal to be examined deprives the employer of a chance to determine conclusively whether the employee is impaired, thereby relieving the employer of some of the burden of proof he would otherwise bear. For example, a two-week disciplinary suspension of a telephone company worker was upheld because the employee had not submitted to a doctor's examination after his supervisor detected symptoms of intoxication; the employee claimed that his wobbly physical state was due to acidosis, a metabolic disorder. The arbitrator wrote:

> Arrangements were made to have a doctor verify either the grievant's claimed condition of acidosis, or the employer's allegation of [being] under the influence, or perhaps even some other undisclosed condition. Rather than allow this diagnosis to be made, the grievant absented himself, thereby denying the parties the ability to resolve the matter by competent medical authority.
>
> . . .
>
> Union counsel is . . . correct when he alleges the employer has not proven beyond a reasonable doubt the grievant was under the influence of alcohol. However, I must examine why the employer could not bring the type of conclusive proof that would have rendered these proceedings moot.
>
> . . .
>
> . . . [When the grievant] absented himself . . . and denied the employer the right to obtain a medical determination, the burden of proof took a significant shift to the grievant, as he in effect resorted to self help.[15]

In a similar case, an arbitrator upheld the disciplinary suspension of an employee who declined to visit the company doctor for a blood test after his foreman observed him walking and talking erratically:

> The clinching fact in this dispute is [the grievant's] refusal to go to the company doctor for a sobriety test. The grounds for this refusal were alleged inadequate treatment for an injury sometime earlier . . . [although] no evidence was introduced to indicate incompetence or bias. . . . What the foreman was doing was offering him a chance to clear himself of the charge in a manner that would leave no room for doubt and would have made the subsequent grievance and arbitration unnecessary. [The grievant] refused. In doing so, he assumed the burden of proof of his own innocence. . . . The presumption must therefore be in favor of the foremen, whose . . . judgment was that he was under the influence of intoxicants.[16]

Union Representation During Testing

Arbitrators have also proven unsympathetic to the argument that an employee is entitled to have union representation when taking a test. In one case a steel plant worker who was asked by the plant patrol to take a breath analyzer test when he reported for work demanded to have the shop steward present. When the plant patrol refused, the employee went home and filed a grievance, claiming that he was improperly denied admission and asking to be made whole for lost wages. The grievance cited a contract provision affording union representation to any employee "who is summoned to meet in an enclosed office with a supervisor for the purpose of discussing possible disciplinary action." The arbitrator held:

> [The grievant] was not being asked to meet with any supervisor or to talk to anyone about possible disciplinary action. He was being given an opportunity by the plant patrol officer to prove by a breathalyzer test that he was not under the influence of alcohol and was fit to enter the plant and go to work.
>
> . . .
>
> . . . The company's evidence does not prove conclusively that [the grievant] was under the influence of alcohol when he attempted to enter the plant gate. But the evidence does show that there were reasonable grounds for the patrolmen to suspect that he had been drinking . . . and to refuse him admission unless he proved his sobriety through a breathalyzer test.[17]

The Chain of Custody of Test Evidence

When blood samples or other laboratory samples are secured, the union may challenge the test results by demanding that the employer prove the integrity of the chain of custody of the evidence. In general, arbitrators appear willing to accept in evidence the report of a qualified, independent testing laboratory without requiring the appearance of laboratory personnel as witnesses (although such personnel have sometimes appeared to explain the tests); the validity of the testing procedure may be presumed once the sample reaches the laboratory. (In drug cases, arbitrators are wont to scrutinize testing procedures more closely, perhaps because identifying drugs is often a more complex task than identifying alcohol; see "Substance Identification" in Chapter 6). But the handling of samples before they reach the laboratory is often a crucial issue in arbitration.

A five-day suspension of a mill worker accused of being intoxicated was overturned by an arbitrator in part because the blood test had been compromised in the arbitrator's eyes by lax handling of the blood sample. The union and employer had previously agreed that in such cases a shop steward and employer representative would jointly oversee the drawing of the sample and would jointly mail it to a medical center for analysis.

> This was not done in this case. In fact, the night superintendent [of the company] testified that he took the blood test to his home, kept it in the refrigerator all evening, brought it back to the plant in the morning, laid it in a box where the outgoing mail was to be picked up at 1:00 . . . in the afternoon. That blood sample was in the company's mail room for approximately three of four hours where anyone could have tampered with it.[18]

In a related case, a discharge was upheld for drinking on the job, despite the union's contention that the contents of the employee's cup, which had been sent to the laboratory for analysis, could have been altered after being taken from the grievant:

> The company did indeed take the cup into its custody and sent it to an independent laboratory. The [arbitration] board simply cannot believe that someone in management poured liquor into the cup. The good faith of the laboratory surely is not a problem. It had nothing to gain or lose by tampering with the contents.[19]

The criterion would seem to be whether a reasonable amount of diligence and normal care were taken in the handling and processing of the sample. Good faith handling is presumed unless there is evidence to the contrary, and the company's burden of proof does not necessarily include the burden of affirmatively demonstrating the security of the sample at every stage of the chain of custody.

Interpreting Blood Test Results

The results of tests for the presence of alcohol in the blood—either by drawn blood sample or by breath or urine analysis—are referred to as the "Blood Alcohol Concentration" (BAC) and are expressed as a percentage. A result of 0.10 means that alcohol constitutes one-tenth of a percent of the blood serum in the sample. The BAC increases with the number of drinks consumed. Table 1 shows, for persons of various weights, the BAC levels produced by drinking 80-proof liquor. One drink of liquor is approximately equivalent to four ounces of wine or twelve ounces of beer. (The heavier the person, the more drinks are required to produce the same BAC.) The higher the concentration of alcohol in the blood, the more pronounced will be the effects on the drinker's behavior, motor coordination, speech and thought.

Table 1. Blood alcohol concentration in relation to body weight and alcohol intake

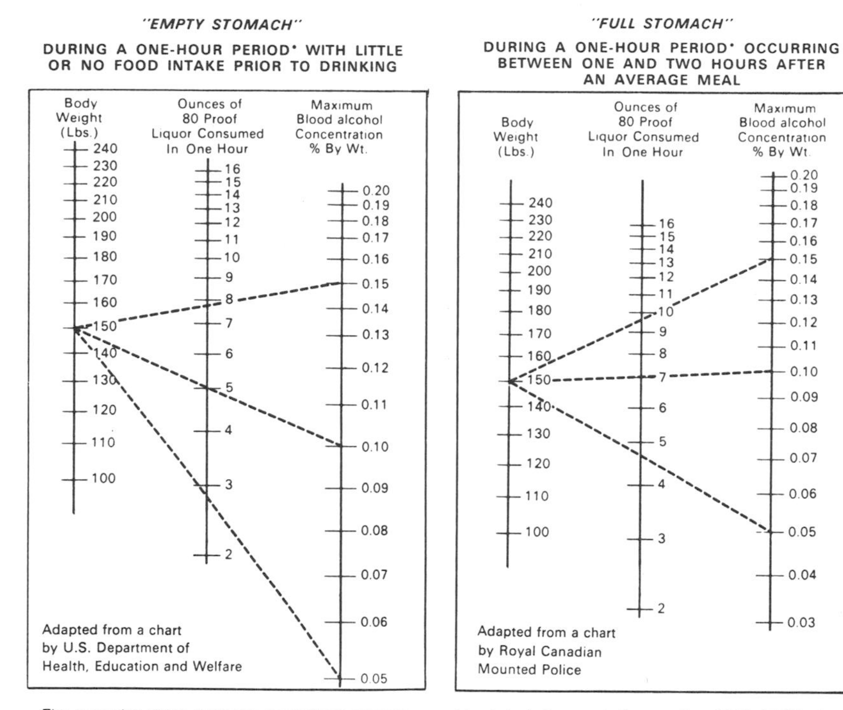

The examples above show the approximate *average* amount of 80 proof liquor a 150-pound person would have to consume in a one-hour period to reach 0.10%, the percentage-weight of alcohol in the bloodstream that is presumptive of intoxication.

To determine the approximate average number of ounces of 80 proof liquor needed in a one-hour period to reach 0.10%, draw a line from BODY WEIGHT to 0.10%. The line will intersect the average number of ounces needed to produce 0.10%. Follow the same procedure to determine the amount of liquor needed to reach other blood-alcohol concentrations, such as 0.05%, 0.15%, etc.

Charts show *rough averages only*. Many factors affect the rate of alcohol absorption into the bloodstream. Amount of food consumed, kind of food and drink consumed, and percentage of fatty tissue in the body, for examples, can vary blood-alcohol concentration values.

*The rate of elimination of alcohol from the bloodstream is approximately 0.015% per hour. Therefore, subtract 0.015% from blood-alcohol concentration indicated on above charts for each hour after the start of drinking.

Source: Reprinted from a booklet entitled *The Drunk Driver May Kill You*, published by Allstate Insurance Co.

An authority on the physiology of intoxication has described the progressive impairment caused by extremely high concentrations of alcohol:

> At 0.20 percent . . . the entire motor area of the brain is profoundly affected. The individual tends to assume a horizontal position; he needs help to walk or undress. At 0.30 percent, from the presence of a pint of whisky in the body, . . . the drinker has little comprehension of what he sees, hears or feels; he is stuporous. At 0.40 percent, perception is obliterated; the person is in a coma, he is anesthetized. At 0.60 or 0.70 percent, the lowest, most primitive levels of the brain controlling breathing and heartbeat cease to function and death ensues.[20]

Use of Motor Vehicle Code BAC Standards

Although the BAC scale is widely used, there is no universally agreed-upon point at which a person may be deemed substantially impaired by alcohol. A common practice in industry is to adopt the BAC standard used in the motor vehicle code of the state in which the employer is located, a practice which particularly commends itself where the employees are using motorized equipment or other dangerous machinery. Under many state codes, a level of 0.10 percent is considered the point of "intoxication" for drivers, although levels as low as 0.05 percent may define "impairment," a lesser offense. The effects of the various levels on a driver's chances of having an accident, as calculated by the New York State Department of Motor Vehicles, are shown in Table 2.

It has been decided by an arbitrator that if a company rule prohibits the employee from being "under the influence" but sets no specific BAC, the 0.10 percent standard, where embodied in the state code, may be presumed to apply:

> In the absence of a plant-wide minimum score being specified in the rules themselves, I conclude that both sides must have intended to rely upon the only other objective criterion readily available—the [state] driver standard. The statutory standard has attempted to draw a line at a point where the test itself supplies an accurate reflection of individual capacity, and the judgemental, coordination and physical demands and the safety considerations of operating a motor vehicle are not unrelated to those applicable in a typical factory situation.[21]

Table 2. Blood alcohol concentration and automobile accident probability

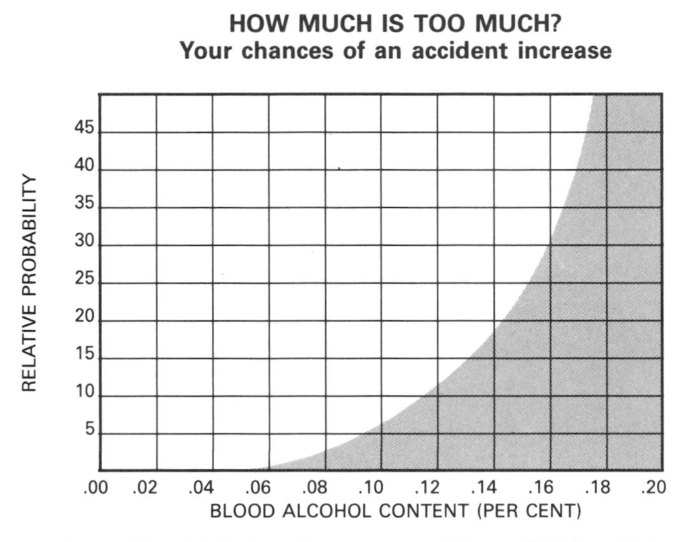

Source: New York State Department of Motor Vehicles, Division of Safety Program Coordination.

Dispute Concerning the Weight Accorded the BAC

Another arbitrator has held that the statutory standard should apply, but only as interpreted by the state courts:

> [T]he company is not required to adopt the views of the courts of the state . . . as to the meaning of "under the influence of intoxicants" insofar as disciplinary rules are involved. But the meaning adopted by the courts is presumptively a reasonable meaning and one upon which an employee may rely unless he is advised otherwise.[22]

The arbitrator here found that a BAC of 0.13 was not just cause for discharge because state courts had ruled that a driver could not be considered "under the influence" unless he was operating his vehicle less safely than he would otherwise, regardless of the amount of alcohol in his blood.

Similarly, an employee who admitted having drunk 24 cans of beer the night before reporting for work and who registered a BAC of more than 0.16 was reinstated on the ground that test results need to be corroborated by observable manifestations of diminished capability. The arbitator wrote:

> The test result merely establishes a presumption that [the grievant] was "under the influence." It is a rebuttable presumption, and nothing more. It does not *prove* that he was so "under the influence" that he was unable to work. It is well known that people have highly individual tolerances for alcohol. . . . [A]n individual who has been a heavy drinker for a substantial period of time may well develop a much higher tolerance for alcohol, that is, a greater ability to function well despite large intake.
>
> . . .
>
> . . . [The test] is not accurate for the teetotaler; it is not accurate for the heavy drinker. It is a measure of the average person's tolerance, but it is of limited value for the extremes.[23]

The validity of the BAC as a reliable indicator was also called into question in a case in which the two grievants had reported for work in a boisterous fashion and were given a breath test several hours later. The results were 0.05 and 0.08, but an expert witness testified that had the test been administered at the time the grievants reported, the results would have been much higher—as much as 0.10 and 0.17 respectively (see discussion below of the alcoholism metabolism rate). The arbitrator held that

> boisterousness alone may not be sufficient [as] an indication that grievants were indeed under the influence of alcohol . . . unless it took an extreme form, and that is not indicated here. . . . The rule requires that an employee be *under* the influence of alcohol—that is the influence must be more than a merely detectable one, it must be an appreciable influence which adversely affects the capability of the employee to competently perform his or her job duties in a safe manner. . . .
>
> . . .
>
> . . . [T]he objective test results . . . should be compared against the subjective manifestations. This time they are not in agreement with one another. Because the subjective manifestations indicate that [the grievants] were not under the influence at the time they reported to work, I conclude that at that time they would have fallen on the exceptional side of the statistical line.[24]

Dispute Concerning "Under the Influence"

While there is obviously some dispute about the weight to be attached to the BAC as proof that the grievant was under the influence, there is little doubt that high levels prove conclusively that the employee has been drinking recently and has yet to metabolize all of the alcohol. A readiness to disregard the test results could become a license for "heavy drinkers" to report to work with a large amount of alcohol still in their systems, which surely is not the intent of the rules being enforced. Moreover, some would argue that the presence of any amount of alcohol in the blood should be deemed to render an employee "under the influence," because, as has often been shown, even small amounts cause measurable deterioration in such functions as reaction time and judgment.

There is, to be sure, a debate between those who consider "under the influence" to mean completely or largely impaired and those who construe it to mean impaired to any degree. There is no doubt, however, that such issues are obviated when the company rules or clear practices embody a specific BAC, even if it is less than 0.10. A three-day suspension was upheld in the case of a railroad switchman whose BAC proved to be 0.05. The arbitrator found that

> [l]ong established policy calls for a warning and a work record demerit with a showing of 0.01 percent on the alcohol blood level test, and suspension or discharge for results showing a higher level of blood alcohol.[25]

Use of Metabolic Calculations

Often a blood test is not administered until some hours after the supervisors notice that an employee appears to be affected by alcohol. In those intervening hours the body will have metabolized some of the alcohol; as a result, the BAC will be lower than at the time the employee was first observed. However, it is possible to estimate what the BAC was at that time by making use of the relatively standard rate at which the body metabolizes alcohol—a decrease in the BAC of approximately 0.01 to 0.02 for every hour after drinking stops. An employee who, for example, registers 0.05 when the sample is drawn may be shown by extrapolation to have been well over 0.10 several hours earlier. Such calculations can also be used to deduce the approximate time at which the drinking occurred.

Testimony by a physician or laboratory scientist that relies upon the metabolism rate has been considered persuasive by arbitrators. In the case of a steel mill employee who was discharged after causing serious injury to himself, the arbitrator, in upholding the discipline, ruled that the metabolism rate evidence tended to prove that the grievant had been drinking while at work:

> A blood sample taken from the grievant at 4:00 PM . . . was analyzed. . . . The analysis showed 0.26 percent of ethyl alcohol in [the grievant's] blood. The arbitrator was convinced by the testimony of [the laboratory representative] . . . that to have 0.26 percent ethyl alcohol in the blood at 4:00 PM would have required a content of 0.32 percent at 1:00 PM [when the grievant was driven to work by a fellow employee] . . . [and] that a person with that degree of alcohol in his blood at 1:00 PM would have obviously been lacking in judgment, his reflexes slow and his speech slow and incoherent.
>
> This evidence, which the arbitrator deems reliable, strongly corroborates the company's contention that *scientifically* the grievant would have had to drink after 2:15 PM [when he reported for work] . . . to be in the condition reflected by the blood tests. It is true that the evidence is circumstantial, but it fits in with the fact that several co-employees testified that at 2:15 PM [the grievant] was able to walk through the gate, . . . go to the bath house, talk to [a supervisor] and was said by co-employees not to be visibly under the influence of alcohol.[26]

The alcohol metabolism rate was also an important factor in the discharge of a railroad machinist who was injured in a collision between two locomotives. On the way to the hospital, the grievant's foreman detected alcohol on the machinist's breath; a blood test revealed a BAC of 0.18. Despite the supervisor's observation and the test result, the grievant denied that he had consumed alcoholic beverages while on duty or immediately before reporting for duty. The tribunal which heard the case reasoned as follows:

> [W]e have before us evidence indicating a substantial amount of alcohol in the employee's bloodstream at approximately 7:45 PM.
>
> The claimant had reported for duty at 3:00 PM, and the accident occurred at approximately 5:30 PM. Thus, the blood alcohol report strongly indicates that—given the rate of decrease in the system—the employee was in a state of intoxication when he reported for duty.[27]

It should be borne in mind that, owing to individual variations, metabolism rate calculations yield only broad time estimates. Therefore, in most situations such calculations should be regarded as suggestive and corroborative evidence rather than as conclusive proof.

6

Medical and Technical Evidence in Drug Cases

Substance Identification

Unlike cases concerning alcohol, arbitrations about drugs often present difficult factual issues, centering upon the nature of the chemical substance in question. While alcohol is readily identifiable, even by laymen, and its effects generally recognizable, the presence of drugs, particularly the so-called "street drugs," is not as easily verified. Thus, many cases turn upon the identity of the substance the employee purportedly possessed, used or sold.

Expert Testimony

The parties often make use of expert witnesses. The need for expert witnesses to testify in hearings relating to drugs has given rise to a new specialty, which has been called "forensic psychopharmacology." The forensic psychopharmacologist offers expert opinion on the properties of various substances and the effects upon those persons who ingest them. Psychology Professor Ronald K. Siegel of the University of California at Los Angeles, an authority on drug use, has remarked that "[t]he primary goal of forensic psychopharmacology is to educate the trier of fact. . . . [H]e is not an advocate in the adversary system and his role is simply to inform."

However, the arbitrator's first task may be to decide who is qualified to testify in this capacity, since, as Professor Siegel points out, "[t]here are no absolute standards for qualifications as an expert witness in drug abuse" partly because of "the failure of the drug abuse field itself to define criteria for expert knowledge." The courts, he notes, have accepted as drug abuse experts a wide range of professionals, including law enforcement officers, chemists, toxicologists, laboratory technicians—even retired pharmacists. Physicians have often been accepted even though they lacked any special training in pharmacology or psychiatry.[1]

The upsurge in drug abuse has by now created a sizable corps of specialists in that field—including researchers, laboratory analysts, clinicians and administrators of treatment programs. Often such persons are called upon to testify as to the identification of the substance that the grievant is charged with using or possessing. Identification of the drug may be critical, depending upon the language of the rule which the grievant is charged with violating and the grievant's line of defense. Under some state laws, for example, marijuana has been defined as the plant *Cannabis sativa,* even though there are two other related species which produce the same effect. Some defendants in criminal cases have used experts to argue that the substance found in their possession belonged not to the legally proscribed cannabis but to one of the other variants.

Use of Commercial Testing Kits

The so-called "three species defense" may be too specious to prevail in the arbitral forum, but in one instance an arbitrator upheld a grievance because the employer failed to demonstrate conclusively that the substance in the employee's possession was "marijuana" within the meaning of federal law. The grievant had been discharged for violating a plant rule against contraband, defined as "all federally controlled drugs not authorized by a licensed physician." Plant guards, using specially trained dogs, discovered in the employee's car marijuana seeds, which were identified by a company official using a commercial testing kit. Referring to U.S. government drug regulations, the arbitrator concluded:

> [T]he seeds of the marijuana plant are not considered to be federally controlled if the seeds are sterile and incapable of germination. Although [a] witness for the employer . . . testified that he had conducted a test with a field kit which showed the seeds tested positive for cannabis resin, this does not in any way establish that the seeds were capable of germination.

> The logical conclusion therefore is that the employer has failed to prove by clear and convincing evidence that the grievant was in possession of a federally controlled substance or in possession of a substance which was regulated by the plant rules. . . . It would seem to me that absent a rule which had been clearly communicated to the employees that possession of any kind of marijuana seeds would subject the employee to discharge then the employer must show that the substance found is a controlled substance which violates the plant rule.[2]

In a similar case, a chief of security at a factory had used a commercial test kit to determine that seeds and leaves found on the premises were marijuana. The union, however, objected that there is no compelling evidence of the existence of marijuana because "the tests were not conducted by an expert."

The arbitrator noted that the test kit was widely used by police departments and security personnel and that it required the user merely to observe the changes in color of the test solution. The security chief had been "tested for color-blindness before the incident and was not found to be color-blind." Moreover, he had watched testing being done by the police. The arbitrator concluded that, on the whole, the company's "investigation was fair and thorough and provided just cause for the termination" of the two grievants.[3]

Presence at the Hearing

Even where expert analysis is performed, the evidence may not stand up in an arbitration unless the experts themselves—and not just their reports—are produced. In one case, an employee was arrested at the plant gate and searched by the police, who found several hand-rolled cigarettes and foil tubes containing vegetable matter. The samples were sent to the state crime laboratory, which returned a report stating that they contained marijuana and hashish respectively. The arbitrator, however, held:

> There is here absent direct evidence of a persuasive and convincing character that the material or substances grievant had in his possession were narcotics, either marijuana or hashish.

The samples themselves were not produced at the arbitration hearing, and

> [n]either of the two identifying technicians, was called to testify. They were not made available for cross-examination as to their

> qualifications, competence, and findings, although the laboratory is located but some fifteen miles [away]. The copy of the laboratory report hardly qualifies as a record *of the company* made in the usual and ordinary conduct of its business.[4]

The arbitrator ordered the grievant reinstated, although without back pay, because the employee failed to cooperate with the employer's investigation.

Eye-Witness Lay Testimony

The identification of marijuana is more complex when there is no sample to be tested and the employer relies on the eye-witness account of a lay observer. An arbitrator upheld the discharge of several employees for violating a plant rule against using narcotics after a boiler shop foreman testified that he had observed the men engaged in a "ritual" associated with marijuana. They were passing a cigarette around in an alleyway:

> After each puff, the smoker allegedly would hold the cigarette under his nose and savor the smoke which drifted up to his nose.[5]

The foreman also testified that he detected the odor of marijuana in the air. "[I]t would almost intoxicate you," he said. The foreman said that he had learned to identify the smell of marijuana smoke by attending a training session.

In another case, a main witness, a night supervisor, asserted that he was able to identify what the grievants were puffing because he had once smoked marijuana himself; he described the odor as "bitter" and resembling that of "burning cabbage." It was perhaps an unusual way to claim expert status, but it convinced the arbitrator:

> His ability to know and perceive what he detected with his own eyes and sense of smell could hardly have been better. Having smoked marijuana himself at one time, he was well aware of its aroma and the appearance of a marijuana "joint."[6]

Despite the failure of the employer to produce the "joint" the employees allegedly smoked—the supervisor had testified that in appearance it "definitely wasn't a Winston filter tip cigarette"—the arbitrator found that the discharge was for just cause. In so doing, he evidently relied heavily upon what he regarded as suspicious circumstances: the employees were discovered inside a compactor with cardboard sheets apparently set against the sides to make seats.

The "unmistakable and unforgettable" odor of marijuana, along with two employees' unexplained presence in an unheated plant loft on a cold night, was the basis for the decision in another case. Here the supervisor who discovered the two grievants claimed to have learned the art of marijuana smoke detection from a one-session drug control course. The employer introduced as an exhibit an "awareness wafer," simulating the smell of the drug, which had been used in the course:

> Because of the pungent odors emitted by the unchallenged sample disc of marijuana, [one] must take judicial notice that indeed there is a distinctive odor [from marijuana]. It is entirely reasonable and logical to assume that the foreman, having been trained concerning the characteristic odors of marijuana, would have detected its presence in this place.

The arbitrator credited this testimony despite his finding that one of the pair was puffing not marijuana but a cigar—a smoking article which has been known to give off rather pungent fumes itself. A key factor was the following curious venue:

> Now, it is fully established by the evidence in this record that the grievants on the night in question had placed themselves in a highly, if not totally, compromising position. On the "coldest night of the year" they had gone more than a quarter of a mile to a point of retreat which was without heat and utterly unattractive in every conceivable way, entirely remote from their places of work.[7]

The cigar smoker was reinstated without back pay, while the discharge of his workmate was upheld.

A 30-day suspension for four employees who allegedly smoked marijuana in a company car in the plant parking lot was upheld by an arbitrator in a case which also turned upon identification by smell. The four were surprised in the car by supervisors:

> When the doors were opened a gush of smoke came out with a smell of burning leaves to it—a sweet smell.[8]

One of the supervisors testified that he was able to recognize it as marijuana because of previous training in drug problems.

In another case, however, a supervisor's testimony that he smelled marijuana smoke as he approached two employees on their lunch break was insufficient to persuade an arbitrator to uphold a half-day suspension for the two men. The men were standing across the street from their workplace, not far from a commercial baking plant. The union introduced evidence to show that marijuana can have a variety of smells and that the neighboring factory often produced strong odors. The arbitrator found the company's case inadequate—but primarily because it did not show that marijuana had impaired the men's ability to work:

> Perhaps this deficiency could or would have been overcome if the company had obtained additional evidence that either the employees had substantially or extensively smoked marijuana on their lunch break, or that it had caused a determinable or noticeable effect on their physical or mental processes or had affected them in such a way that they could not perform their work satisfactorily. . . .
>
> . . .
>
> Even if we were to concede credibility to [the supervisor's smelling] or detection of the marijuana odor, the company has failed to establish if the cigarette was smoked by the two fully or extensively, as opposed to only a quick puff, which could raise a question of how extensively they were under the influence or affected by it; we say this keeping in mind the total context of the case and also the fact that they were off the company premises.[9]

The two employees were reinstated with back pay.

Validity of Observations and Identifications

In all of the cases just reviewed, the arbitrators were willing to credit a supervisor's ability to detect marijuana smoke by its smell, even though most of the witnesses could claim no expertise apart from rather casual experience—such as their own use of the drug! There is reason to doubt whether the average, untrained human nose can reliably detect the presence of marijuana. As Professor Siegel of UCLA has remarked, "Such discrimination is . . . open to question, as there are few good experiments pertaining to such olfactory abilities in man."[10] This caveat is particularly important if there are odors competing with the purported marijuana smoke. In two of the cases discussed, the identification of marijuana by smell was accepted, even though in one case cigar smoke was present and, in the other case, the aromas of a commercial baking plant were present.

It is perhaps significant that two of the witnesses who testified that they knew marijuana when they smelled it gave diametrically opposite descriptions: in one case the smoke was described as "bitter," in the other as "sweet." The critical factor in some of these examples may have been that the identification was backed by the observation of furtive behavior—employees discovered in remote or unusual locations without any evident reason for being there. In several instances, the testimony most damaging to the grievant was probably the account of the "ritual" conventionally associated with marijuana smoking: a hand-rolled cigarette being passed around ceremonially.

Furtive behavior and "ritual" are corroborating indicators of possible marijuana use, but they are far from conclusive. For one thing, so-called "street drugs" are often not what they appear to be or even what the user thinks them to be. A survey of laboratory analyses of street drugs, published in 1977, revealed that only about half of the more than 6,000 samples tested contained precisely the substance which they were alleged to contain; in some instances, the sample revealed a different drug, the alleged drug plus others or no drugs at all.[11] (Thirty-five purported samples of marijuana contained none.) It is possible, therefore, that an employee who participates in what seems to be a marijuana-smoking ritual may be doing nothing more than passing a hand-rolled cigarette around with his workmates. Consequently, where the identification of the substance is critical to enforcement of a disciplinary rule, care should be taken to ensure that the evidence is sufficient to make the correct identification, in light of what is known about the idiosyncrasies of street drugs. This is especially important where the rules call for summary discharge for the first offense.

Prescription drugs, which are issued by manufacturers under generic or brand names, are generally easier to identify, but there have been cases in which the identity of a prescription drug was at issue. In one case, the issue turned upon the admissibility of technical evidence tendered by the employer.

The grievant had been discharged for violation of a plant rule against "the illegal use of drugs." He had been observed attempting to dispose of a vial of pills after being injured in an accident in the plant; company officials retrieved the pills and had them analyzed. At the arbitration hearing, the employer presented a report, signed by a forensic scientist at the state crime laboratory, which concluded that the pills contained a tranquilizer. The union objected that the report was inadmissible.

The arbitrator agreed with the union. He noted that the pills had previously been tested by another laboratory, which reported that they contained not a tranquilizer but an amphetamine. In reinstating the grievant, the arbitrator wrote:

> While as a general rule the hearsay rule is not strictly applied in arbitration matters, in view of the prior history of the testing of the pills by the company, the key nature of this proferred evidence, and the failure of the company to produce the author of the report for cross-examination as to qualifications, competence and findings, I have concluded that the report should not be admitted into evidence.[12]

Since establishing the nature of the drug was essential to a finding of illegal possession, the company did not meet its burden of proof.

Proving Impairment by Drugs

The mere possession of marijuana and other illegally possessed substances will usually subject the employee to discipline, but there are many drugs which are lawfully possessed and used by employees: over-the-counter drugs, drugs prescribed for them by a physician and the so-called "look-alike" drugs, which resemble prescription pills but contain non-controlled substances such as caffeine, often in high doses. Nevertheless, abuse of these drugs can be just as deleterious to a person's health and ability to work as illegal substances. Indeed, a report by the U.S. General Accounting Office in 1982 found that prescription drugs "dominate the statistics" dealing with drug emergencies and fatalities. Nearly three-quarters of deaths attributed to drugs by medical examiners in 1980 were linked to prescription drugs.[13]

In a discipline case involving a legal drug, the question is not the simple one of whether the employee possessed the drug or used any of it. Rather, the question is whether he used it in a manner which caused impairment and whether the employee can be held accountable for the impairment.

Those issues were presented by the discharge of a fork-lift operator who appeared to be acting abnormally when he reported for work. The foreman and other company witnesses testified that the grievant "was in a staggery and unbalanced condition and that his speech was slurred and thick-tongued."

He was sent home and ultimately discharged for violation of a plant rule against "reporting to work under influence of intoxicants or drugs." The union defended the employee by attributing his condition to taking tranquilizers and a sleeping pill, both medications prescribed for a him by a doctor.

The arbitrator upheld the discharge, reasoning that, however the condition had been produced, the testimony established a violation of the rule inasmuch as the grievant was clearly unfit to work:

> The uniform testimony of the several witnesses . . . leads to the only logical conclusion that grievant was not physically [or] mentally capable of performing his assigned duties of driving a lift truck.
>
> The essence of the offense . . . is the voluntary creation of the condition by the ingestion of intoxicants or drugs.

The arbitrator gave little weight to the grievant's assertion that the condition was excusable because it was produced by a prescription drug; the arbitrator pointed out that in a note submitted as an exhibit by the union the prescribing physician had stated that, if taken as directed, the medicines "should not make a person drunk-like." The arbitrator concluded:

> The fact that the pills were prescribed by a doctor would not lessen the offense if grievant voluntarily consumed an overdose in order to induce a euphoric state. The prescription called for one [tranquilizer pill] three times a day and a disregard of this direction, producing a condition which incapacitated grievant from performing his assigned job, is the equivalent of the proscribed conduct of "reporting to work under the influence of intoxicants or drugs."

The final reason for upholding the discharge was the grievant's disciplinary record; three times he had been disciplined for similar conduct within 15 months. That record, the arbitrator held, "led the company to the reasonable conclusion that the propensity of the grievant to render himself unfit for work by the use of intoxicants or drugs was not correctable."[14]

It is noteworthy that the tranquilizer in question, Tranxene, is listed in the standard *Physicians' Desk Reference*[15] with the following warning: "Patients on Tranxene should be cautioned against engaging in hazardous occupations requiring mental alertness, such as operating dangerous machinery, including motor vehicles."[15] Drowsiness was listed as the most common side effect. This would suggest that when drugs like Tranxene are involved, the normal prescription dosage might, in fact, be responsible for the behavioral symptoms exhibited by the grievant. The arbitrator can take judicial notice—with appropriate acknowledgement in the opinion—of the information about the drug contained in such reference works as the *PDR*, which is based on the manufacturers' descriptions.

Previous Drug Abuse

Where an employee has a record of drug abuse, it may not be necessary for the employer to prove conclusively that a subsequent incident of unfitness to work was caused by drugs in order to discharge him. In one case an arbitrator upheld the discharge of an employee, twice suspended for drug-related misconduct, who was found by the foreman asleep at a radial drill press:

> After some effort the foreman was able to rouse grievant but sent him home because in the foreman's opinion grievant was not in a fit condition to work. Grievant protested that he was able to work and that he was not under the influence of drugs. . . .
>
> . . .
>
> If in fact grievant was under the influence of drugs . . . his discharge was unquestionably proper under the "last chance" provisions of the [last] suspension. Even assuming that he was not, and that he was merely fatigued on that occasion because of other personal problems, the fact remains that he was in a deep sleep, at 2 PM, while his machine was operating. Such conduct in and of itself constitutes cause for discharge.[16]

Determining the Cause of Impairment

An arbitrator sometimes faces the task of deciding whether abnormal behavior is attributable to alcohol, to drugs or to both. Typical is the case in which a barber in a state institution reported for work in a wobbly condition and was discharged for being under the influence of alcohol. The employee contended that the behavior observed by his supervisors was produced not by alcohol but by the medications he was taking to relieve a central nervous system disorder. The grievant had recently been released from the hospital, and he furnished a note from his doctor stating that he was being treated with, among other drugs, Valium and Tuinal—both of which are central nervous system depressants (see Appendix A).

The arbitrator decided that discharge was too severe because of the grievant's unblemished work record but that there was just cause for a suspension. Noting that the company doctor and others also had detected the smell of alcohol on the grievant's breath, the arbitrator wrote:

> The grievant does not deny that he exhibited abnormal behavior when he reported for work. . . . He does not deny that he staggered, lacked coordination and that his speech was thick and slurred. These are symptoms which are commonly recognized as being associated with the consumption of alcohol.
>
> . . .
>
> . . . In all candor, it is hard for the arbitrator to believe that the adverse reaction of the drugs and/or his disease took place at the very same time that the grievant consumed alcohol. Why at that very time—why not at a time when the grievant does not have alcohol on his breath?
>
> . . .
>
> . . . [T]he arbitrator is fully satisfied that the grievant did not suffer any adverse reaction from the drugs or his disease after his release from [the hospital] until . . . the odor of alcohol was detected on his breath. This is convincing evidence that his abnormal behavior was caused by consumption of alcohol.[17]

In a related case, a delivery truck driver with an excellent work history was discharged for appearing at the end of his shift in an incoherent state. The employer accused him of being "under the influence of alcoholic beverages or narcotics including hallucinogens while on duty." The arbitrator confessed:

> I have had a problem in concluding whether grievant's uncharacteristic behavior was caused by alcohol or drugs, [or] some combination of the two, and, if by drugs alone, whether by some innocent mixing of them.
>
> . . .
>
> . . . [M]y life of experience causes me to doubt that one with no drinking history on the job or elsewhere, with a flawless job performance record, and with higher than average job accomplishments, would suddenly get dog drunk on the job knowing he had to check out and be observed by his supervisors. Only compelling addiction or stupidity could produce that sort of conduct and grievant has not been accused of either.
>
> I think the chances are greater that there was a culpable mixing of drugs and alcohol that produced a wholly unexpected result. . . . [W]e do not have to be scientists to know that light mixtures of some drugs with limited alcohol produces unexpected results in some people.
>
> . . .

> . . . [The] grievant should be reinstated . . . without any back pay . . . since . . . grievant's actions, though producing unexpected results, [were] punishable.[18]

Disputes Over the Significance of Symptoms

The employer may seek to make its case by establishing a behavioral syndrome suggestive of drug use, and the union may seek to show that the symptoms were caused by illness, fatigue or the untoward effects of routine medications. In such a case, an airline flight attendant was discharged for "being under the influence of an intoxicant" while on duty. Several of the grievant's fellow flight attendants, testifying for the company, said that they observed that she was unsteady and at times seemed dazed. Some of the witnesses testified that she seemed to be "on drugs."

No medical tests were performed, but the company argued that "arbitral precedent both on this property and elsewhere holds that in cases involving intoxication, the direct observation[s] of lay witnesses are adequate to establish the condition and medical testing is not required." The union contended that the company had failed to meet its burden of proving that the grievant was under the influence of a drug because "other explanations are plausible in accounting for her behavior." It asserted that her condition could have been due to the fact that she had a sleepless night and was feeling flustered because of a late arrival for work. The union insisted that the testimony of the witnesses was not consistent, so that it was incumbent upon the company to produce medical evidence to substantiate the charge of intoxication.

The arbitrator held that the company had put forward a *prima facie* case which the grievant did not credibly rebut by her own testimony:

> Although their words were not the same, the cumulative impact of [the witnesses'] direct observations is overwhelming. The grievant's eyes were described as droopy, glassy, blurry, watery, wandering unfocussed and vacant. Her speech was characterized as slurred, confused, disjointed and incoherent. Her motor functions were depicted as uncoordinated, unbalanced, slow, wobbly, unsteady, unstable, stumbling and swaying. . . .
>
> . . .
>
> Although I agree with the union that each of the incidents of the grievant's work performance is insignificant, if viewed singly

and in isolation, taken together they provide cumulative evidence that the grievant's conduct was indeed unusual and abnormal, and could fairly be characterized as that of a drug-intoxicated person.

. . .

. . . I do not find that the company's case must fail because of the absence of medical evidence in light of the overwhelming nature of its proof, but I suggest that an effort to obtain such evidence might be desirable in a case in which the testimony of the disinterested lay witnesses is less convincing and conclusive.

. . . [The grievant] could not offer any credible evidence to show that her condition was caused by any factor other than intoxication. Her excuses concerning her fatigue, anxiety and semi-comatose condition are simply insufficient to explain her behavior and conduct.

A minority opinion, signed by the union-appointed members of the System Board of Adjustment, objected:

The record is replete with symptoms that establish only a suspicion of intoxication. Suspicion, however, is not enough to prove clearly and convincingly that the grievant was intoxicated as charged. There was no evidence unique to a finding of intoxication, such as the odor of alcohol. (In fact, the board was offered no evidence to decide exactly what symptoms are necessary to prove intoxication.)

. . .

. . . Too numerous are the reasons that eyes may appear glassy, including our harsh environment, slight fatigue and lack of humidity on the aircraft. Appearing unsteady, especially when carrying heavy suitcases and purses, does not prove intoxication.[19]

Abuse of Unknown Substances

In several of the cases discussed above, the arbitrators reached their decisions without ascertaining precisely which substance actually caused the impairment. In one case the question was left open as to whether it was alcohol or drugs; in another there was no determination of which drug was responsible for the drug-intoxication that the arbitrator found to have been proven. This process of reasoning backward—of inferring substance abuse from the employee's behavior without ascertaining which substance was involved—is quite common, because the possible range of abused substances is so large. Moreover, some employees may engage in "polyabuse," the tendency to abuse more than one substance simultaneously or to use drugs in combination with alcohol. (Such abusers are sometimes referred to as "chemical gourmets.") Employers thus have been upheld when discharging employees for abusing an unknown substance.

Arbitrators might do well to consider, however, whether in some circumstances such a charge may be so vague as to deny the grievant "due process." It is difficult to rebut the charge of being under the influence of a substance when no substance is specified; the grievant does not have even the opportunity of pointing to discrepancies between the observed behavior and the known properties of a specific substance. To the extent that the charge is not open to refutation, it may be inherently unfair. Even so staunch an opponent of abuse as the U.S. Drug Enforcement Administration has cautioned:

> It must be kept in mind that the observable effects of drug abuse and overdose are often similar to the symptoms of illness. Such effects as watery or redrimmed eyes, dizziness, runny nose, and slurred speech may be symptoms of common ailments. Therefore, attribution of such symptoms to drug abuse must be done only on the advice of health professionals or where other independent corroboration can be obtained.[20]

No doubt the most accurate way of establishing that an employee is under the influence of drugs would be to perform a chemical test. However, unlike alcohol, for which there are standard breath and urine tests, satisfactory tests for many drugs are not yet available. There are laboratory procedures for detecting the presence in urine of tetrahydrocannabinol (THC), the ingredient which produces the effects associated with marijuana. But the test is too sensitive to furnish useful evidence. In some instances, persons who merely sat in the same vehicle as a marijuana smoker showed traces of THC. Moreover, marijuana smoked weeks earlier may produce a positive test result. In a case in which an employee was alleged to have used marijuana at work or just before coming to work, such a test result would be inconclusive.

Another complicating factor is the absence of an accepted scale, comparable to the blood alcohol content level, for measuring the effect of marijuana upon an individual. In a letter to the medical community in 1983, a group of toxicologists cautioned:

> It is impossible, at present, to establish by urine testing methods that the person [who smoked marijuana] was adversely

> affected by the drug . . . [A] correlation between blood concentrations and possible impairment has not yet been fully established.[21]

The inherent uncertainties in trying to attribute abnormal behavior to drugs suggest that it might be clearer and fairer for employers to discipline for "unfitness to work" or manifest impairment rather than for drug use. Of course, the discipline then would not be summary in nature; a single instance of unfitness presumably would merit a warning or suspension. Still, by holding the employee responsible for repeated instances of "unfitness" according to the dictates of progressive discipline, the ultimate penalty could, in the end, be imposed upon chronic drug abusers.

Classifying Drugs

In assessing an employee's involvement with drugs, it is critical to have a clear understanding of the drug in question. Often the statements about drugs that are made in arbitration lack sufficient precision. In particular, the notion of what is a "narcotic" seems to vary widely. Valium,[22] amphetamines[23] and marijuana[24] have at various times been deemed "narcotics" in arbitrations, although scientific opinion would consider these substances, respectively, a depressant, a central nervous system stimulant and a psycho-active substance usually classed by itself.

In the case discussed under "The Grievant as 'Addict'" in Chapter 4, cocaine was defined as a "stimulant-type narcotic drug."[25] The phrase obscures a crucial distinction: cocaine acts as a central nervous system stimulant akin to the amphetamines. The substances classified by pharmacologists as narcotics are analgesics and are, like heroin and codeine, derivatives of opium or synthetic variants of the opiates.

Misunderstandings may arise from the dichotomy between the legal and pharmacological taxonomies. The legal status of the drug may be ascertained by consulting the regulations formulated pursuant to the Federal Controlled Substances Act (see Appendix C). The pharmacological classification—based upon the drug's effects on the human body—may be determined by consulting the reference works published by medical and pharmaceutical organizations (see Appendix A). If the parties do not present sufficient evidence about the nature of the drug involved in the case, it would seem prudent for arbitrators to take judicial notice by consulting these sources and acknowledging them in the opinion.

Apart from their legal and pharmacological classifications, drugs are sometimes divided into categories according to how liable they are to be abused or to promote dependence. What matters in this distinction is the behavior of individuals toward these substances. Some drugs, including hallucinogens and cocaine, are commonly considered "recreational drugs," because they are most often used episodically as a leisure-time social activity and because physiological dependence has not been demonstrated. However, both substances may figure in "substance use disorders," according to the diagnostic criteria of the American Psychiatric Association (see "Drug Abuse as a Treatable Disorder" in Chapter 2), as may marijuana.

Cocaine

Cocaine has enjoyed a particular vogue as the "caviar" of drugs. Its use is reportedly widespread in some industries, such as sports and advertising, and its popularity is apparently growing at a disturbing rate. The Department of Justice reported that 40 to 48 metric tons of cocaine were illegally imported to the United States in 1980 (to be sold at an ultimate retail price of about $500,000 per kilo), an increase of 50 percent over the previous year. About 5 million Americans are thought to use the drug regularly.

A cocaine "high," induced by nasal inhalation or injection, creates heightened sensibility and a feeling of energy and exhilaration, but the effect is fleeting, lasting perhaps 10 to 30 minutes. Cocaine—unlike heroin, for example—is not the drug of the "dropout." On the contrary, it is commonly used by strongly motivated employees, many of whom believe that it may actually improve their job performance. (Heroin is more prevalent among low-paid workers, even though it costs more than cocaine.)

Because cocaine is distributed along a diffuse network of social acquaintances, employees who use and sell cocaine to one another are less likely than users of other drugs to depend upon underworld connections and to fall afoul of the law. As the French newspaper *Le Monde* reported in an article on the international cocaine fad, "only a tiny minority of cocaine users lacks a regular supply, and their social, cultural, and financial level prohibits them from turning to delinquency."[26] Cocaine has, in fact, become a symbol of high status.

The implications for discipline cases are many. A grievant charged by an employer with violation of a company rule against use of "narcotics" might challenge the discipline on the ground that the rule did not clearly encompass cocaine. He might also argue that a rule against being "under the influence of drugs" does not apply since such a rule is intended to bar workers whose performance has been adversely affected by drugs; in this instance, the employee might argue that performance—measured in terms of stamina or alertness—had actually been enhanced. Moreover, a grievant in an industry where cocaine use is notorious might argue that its use has been implicitly condoned by employers. Employers, in fact, have been known to supply cocaine to employees as an inducement and aid to hard work. The practice dates back to colonial times in South America, when Spanish authorities furnished the drug to Indian miners laboring under arduous conditions. In recent years there have been reports of employers giving cocaine to employees who were asked to work exceptionally long periods of overtime.[27]

A carefully drawn plant rule against the use or possession of "illicit drugs" or "controlled substances" would certainly encompass cocaine, provided that the rule is promulgated clearly and that there is no evidence of condonation by the employer in the past. Such a rule could be upheld on performance grounds, quite apart from the ground of the illegality of the substance, since the "crashing" phase which follows the initial euphoria can produce anxiety and extreme fatigue—conditions detrimental to job safety and effectiveness. The "high" itself can result in impaired judgment, which is particularly dangerous to operators of machinery or vehicles.

When cases do reach arbitration—relatively few have been reported so far[28]—care must be taken to ensure that cocaine's special characteristics are recognized so that those participating in the decisionmaking process do not labor under assumptions that apply to other drugs but not to cocaine.

7

Applying the Rules: Consistency, Clarity and Reasonableness

Consistent Enforcement of Alcohol and Drug Rules

In alcohol and drug cases, as indeed in other types of disciplinary arbitrations, consistency of rule application is an important factor in establishing just cause. An arbitrator, upholding a discharge for being under the influence of alcohol, was impressed by the employer's long record of having taken similar action and noted:

> [The company presented as an exhibit] a list of employees who have been discharged for reporting to work . . . under the influence of alcohol. It is noted that this list . . . extends back [28 years]. The director of industrial relations testified that every person who has been found to be under the influence of alcohol has been discharged. It is difficult to conceive how a company could be more consistent in its application of a rule.[1]

Equal Treatment of Drug and Alcohol Offenders

Arbitrators may discern discriminatory treatment where drug offenders are dealt with more harshly than alcohol offenders. The discharge of a chemical industry worker accused of marijuana possession in the plant was reduced to a two-week suspension because alcohol offenders were treated more leniently. The arbitrator wrote:

> [The company rule] states that "carrying cameras, firearms, weapons, alcohol or illegal drugs onto company property . . . "

> is forbidden. It does not distinguish between these items by stating that one is a more important violation than the others. At the hearing both company and union witnesses testified that alcoholism is dealt with by referral to a clinic and by the use of progressive discipline. Since the company heretofore had not discharged an employee for drug abuse, the union had no reason to believe that a drug problem would be handled differently from alcoholism. . . . [T]here is a large area of disagreement among qualified scientists and doctors on the effects of marijuana. I, therefore, cannot conclude that the use of alcohol on company property is less dangerous than the use of marijuana, or that the referral to a drug abuse program is less effective than the referral to an alcohol abuse program.[2]

Similarly, an arbitrator reinstated (albeit without back pay) an employee in whose clothing a marijuana cigarette was discovered while he was being treated for a chemical burn:

> Unrefuted testimony was given that workers had been sent home from the plant gate, and the job as well, who had obviously consumed alcohol and were under its influence at the time. These latter employees were not subject to discipline while the grievant had been discharged. It is true that the grievant is the first employee discharged for drug possession, but the rule that prohibits the one is the same rule that prohibits the other. Also, the justification for the rule is the avoidance of the problems related to the use of "intoxicants, drugs or hallucinogenic agents" which again puts them in the same category, notwithstanding a difference in their legal status which is a matter at law. While the two acts are technically different, the company's justification for interest in controlling them and the statement of rules tend to equate them. The use of these items has a similar debilitating effect on people, the basic safety problem of concern to the company in both cases. It would thus appear that the company has been inconsistent in the assessment of the hazards involved, and in turn the penalties applied. It is prevention and not punishment that is to be sought in such cases.[3]

In both cases where discriminatory treatment was discerned, the arbitrators attached significance to the absence of evidence that the employee was affected by the marijuana in his possession. In this first case the arbitrator remarked:

> The company . . . presented no testimony that the grievant's smoking on these occasions affected his work in any way. Although the company stated its concern about the possibility of dangerous mistakes caused by the erroneous mixture of chemicals, the grievant did not work in a sensitive area; his job was in the boiler house unloading and shoveling coal.[4]

And the second arbitrator commented:

> Grievant did possess marijuana but no evidence was presented that he had used any of it; in fact, testimony was given that indicated he had not and was functioning in a normal manner while on the job.[5]

Such rulings suggest that the sheer illegality of marijuana possession or use by itself does not amount to just cause for discharge under company rules which lump together alcohol and drugs. Just as the company may be required to show that an employee's performance suffered from the effects of alcohol consumption, it may be required to demonstrate—and not merely presume—the ill effects of drug use.

However, by no means do all arbitrators agree that drug offenders should be treated in a manner similar to alcohol offenders. The discharge of a crane operator for violating a rule against drug or alcohol possession was upheld by an arbitrator who appeared to have accepted the employer's position that drugs—more than alcohol—merited summary discipline:

> The evidence . . . indicates that the employer has not automatically discharged every employee who reported for work under the influence of alcohol or even every employee found in the possession of an alcoholic beverage on the company's premises. The employer has explained this different treatment . . . on the ground that alcoholism is a disease subject to treatment. It will continue the employment of an employee with an alcohol problem if the employee will undertake a program of cure. The employer contends, however, that there is no addiction to the use of marijuana. It is a "social drug" used by choice which has no place in the industrial environment.[6]

Arbitrators have discerned discriminatory treatment where the buyer of a controlled substance at the workplace was not disciplined along with the seller. The discharge of an employee who had become a walking pharmacy for his fellow employees was held to be too severe:

> The grievant . . . was discharged . . . for selling 86 2mg Valium pills to another employee, B——. According to the company the sale took place on the company's premises during working hours and . . . $5.00 exchanged hands . . . .
>
> . . .
>
> . . . These pills he had obtained legitimately with a prescription from his doctor. . . . He also was using other pain killing drugs prescribed by the doctor. He apparently was, by his own admission, bringing in and, it might be said, dispensing other medication on request of fellow employees. These were Anacin, penicillin, as well as the Valium, and B—— said he had bought

> Percodan for a headache. . . .
>
> . . .
>
> . . . B—— by accepting or buying the controlled substance also was in violation of [company rules] and while he was not quite, in my opinion, as guilty as [the grievant] he too should have been disciplined. Since he (B——) wasn't and since [the grievant] had 10 years seniority, I am of the opinion that discharge was too severe a penalty.[7]

The discharge was reduced to a disciplinary layoff of three months with back pay for earnings lost beyond that period.

The Reasonableness of Rules

Whether an offense occurs on or off the premises, the reasonableness of the rule, its application and the discipline meted out under it are viewed by arbitrators in relation to the nature of the industry and the possible hazards created by use of alcohol or drugs. As one arbitrator, upholding a discharge for a first offense of being under the influence of alcohol, commented:

> In view of the fact that the facility . . . is owned by the U.S. Government and engaged in making live ammunition it must be concluded that the rule is reasonable if for no other reason than the nature of the product.[8]

A similar conclusion was reached by an arbitrator upholding a five-day suspension of a civilian employee for possession of marijuana at an Air Force base:

> The arbitrator . . . finds that the possibility of job impairment and the increased risk to the safety of others is . . . readily apparent in a situation where the employer is servicing jet aircraft . . . .[9]

The Employer's Public Image

It is also evident that in drug cases arbitrators weigh carefully the possibility that a grievant's drug involvement may be harmful to the reputation or integrity of the employer. Public employers are often deemed particularly vulnerable. The discharge of a maintenance worker at a state university who had been arrested for selling amphetamines to an undercover detective on campus was upheld by an arbitrator who took note of the sensitive position of a public institution of higher education:

> In determining penalty, I cannot ignore the special responsibility the state university has to its students and their parents. The state is obligated to see that its campuses are not sanctuaries for the drug trade. It is no secret that drugs are a problem on the nation's campuses and on this one, in particular. . . .
>
> Allowing grievant's return to duty would have a negative impact on the orderly operation of the university. It would send the wrong message to the rest of its employees.[10]

The case for adverse effects on the employer must be compelling, however. A public utility worker who sold amphetamines shortly before beginning his employment was discharged when he pleaded guilty to drug charges. He was reinstated by an arbitrator, who reasoned:

> [The grievant's] arrest and conviction carried over to the period of his employment but those occurrences do not create a sufficient link or connection between the illegal conduct and grievant's job or employer–employee relation. The employer's evidence was less than substantial in showing a direct, damaging impact on the manner in which [the grievant] did his work or on the image or legitimate business interests of the company. There is no question but that grievant's offense was both legally and morally wrong but that was a concern for the civil authorities. In the absence of evidence of a more direct, adverse impact on grievant's job performance or damage to the company's image or reputation for public service and integrity, or even the existence of a general drug problem among its employees, the discharge cannot be sustained. In sum, the company's understandable fears remained inchoate.[11]

Even a private employer's argument that it has a "high public profile," readily undermined by employee lawbreaking, will be taken into account. But relatively minor offenses, such as simple possession of marijuana, may not be sufficiently notorious to support the severest discipline. An aircraft component manufacturer in Canada argued that its discharge of an employee convicted of marijuana possession was justified because the criminal court proceeding jeopardized its standing with the public. The arbitrator disagreed:

> Although the company equated its business with the business of Air Canada for the purpose of showing that it had a high public profile similar to Air Canada which could be damaged by employee misconduct, it must be recognized that as a manufacturer of aircraft or aircraft components, the company was one step removed from the very sensitive public position that Air Canada has since Air Canada operates the aircraft which the public uses and therefore many of its employees must deal with the public.

> . . . I accept the company's argument that any adverse publicity which reflects on the quality of the company's product is a serious matter. However, it must be noted that there was no evidence of any real notoriety connected with the [grievant's] offense.[12]

A similar result was reached in a case that did involve a major airline. Because it maintained daily contacts with government regulatory and customs officials, the employer pleaded a special need to deal firmly with employees who were arrested for possession of marijuana:

> The company's decision to discharge (the grievant) is a reflection of its awareness that to look the other way would only serve to encourage similar illegal acts by the other workers and further jeopardize the vital relationship with the various federal and state agencies upon which the company so heavily depends.

The arbitrator gave the claim a sympathetic hearing but ruled:

> It is understandable that the company must preserve its cordial relationships with various governmental agencies, but there is no evidence that a disciplinary penalty less severe than discharge, would result in any impairment of such relationships.[13]

Defining "Intoxication" and Related Alcohol- or Drug-Induced Conditions

The interpretation of employer rules against working while "intoxicated," "inebriated" or "under the influence" of alcohol may give rise to disputes if they lack specificity. As noted in the discussion of technical evidence (Chapters 5 and 6), the notion of "under the influence" is inherently a matter of degree. To be clear-cut, a rule should specify what degree of impairment or blood alcohol concentration (BAC) constitutes "under the influence," And the rule should be widely published, along with the penalties. As one arbitrator has commented:

> The employees are entitled to know the definition of "under the influence of liquor or any alcoholic beverage in areas assigned to the company at any time"; to know what criteria the company intends to use to determine this fact; and to know definitely what the punishment is for a violation of this rule. And all of these things must be known to the employees *before* the company subjects them to capital punishment under . . . said rule.[14]

(The union had argued in this case that "[t]he grievant did not realize that he could drink liquor while off duty, then sleep for several hours, and still be intoxicated the next morning; if he had, he would not have reported to work the next day . . . .")[15]

Since even small amounts of blood alcohol can be shown to produce some deterioration in task performance, a rule tolerating none does not fly in the face of reason, but employees must be fully apprised in advance that such a standard will be applied. Given proper notice and a well-defined BAC standard, an employee's argument that he did not *appear* to be under the influence presumably would carry little weight.

Hourly Rules

The effect of a BAC standard may be blurred, however, by simultaneous enforcement of a rule prohibiting employees from drinking within a certain number of hours before reporting for duty. Rules specifying a period of eight hours or more are common, particularly in the transportation industry. Such rules can create the unfortunate impression that by refraining from consumption of alcohol within the forbidden period, the employee may report to work confident that he is not "under the influence." Yet it can take much longer for alcohol ingested during a session of social or dinner drinking to be fully metabolized by the human body. An employee who reports to work eight hours after such a session may be shocked to find that his blood alcohol test results have led to disciplinary charges.

Pre-duty drinking bans also present enforcement problems. As one arbitrator has noted in an airline dispute involving a 24-hour rule:

> This is a type of rule most difficult, if not impossible, to police and enforce, unless the violation is attended by erratic conduct at or aboard the aircraft, or unless all employees cooperate, particularly when the violations occur in foreign lands several thousand miles from the management base.[16]

In that case, the arbitrator reduced to a suspension the discharge of three flight attendants for drinking during a layover in Tokyo. The arbitrator found that under the employer rules a violation of the 24-hour ban, especially a first offense, was an infraction too minor to merit discharge. He took into account that the grievants seemed not to have shown the effects of drinking. The pilot on the return journey reported that the flight attendants were "neat and pleasant and, in my opinion, did their job in an above average manner. I feel sure the passengers felt the same way."[17]

In a related case, an arbitrator reinstated without back pay a flight attendant accused of violating an airline's 12-hour rule:

> Violation of the 12-hour no-drinking rule is a matter of the most serious import. It may lead not only to damage to customer relations but also to an impairment of safety. All such cases should be severely dealt with. But it is noteworthy that company regulations do not impose a mandatory discharge penalty for this offense. . . . Room is left for judgment and for the weighing of all factors present in the case.[18]

One of the factors weighed by the arbitrator in this case, as in the preceding one, was the absence of clear evidence that the grievant was affected by her drinking—a single glass of champagne—when she reported for work.

Suspicion of Impairment Rules

It may well be simpler to substitute for the hourly rule a requirement that the employee report for work with his faculties unimpaired and that, if his behavior gives rise to reasonable suspicion of impairment, he must be able to show by means of a blood test that he is alcohol-free. Such a requirement, it might be argued, could result in an employee's unwitting commission of what might be termed metabolic misconduct: too slowly dissipating consumed alcohol. That would be unfair inasmuch as individuals cannot easily gauge their BAC. However, the reasonableness requirement, enforceable in arbitration, would assure that blood alcohol did not even become an issue unless there were observable signs of impairment.

If an hourly rule is thought to be necessary as a guideline, then it is prudent to embrace a period long enough to be certain that all alcohol in the bloodstream has been metabolized. Given the variations in the amounts that may be drunk and in human metabolism rates, a period of 24 hours is probably the minimum time span that can be safely recommended—assuming that such an intrusion into an individual's private life is justified by the nature of the job.

Rules on Possession and Use of Alcohol

Under the rules of many employers, possession of alcohol at the workplace is punishable by discharge, even for a first offense, and arbitrators have upheld the enforcement of such rules even where the amount of alcohol was small and the employee had many years of service. In a steel industry case, the arbitrator upheld the discharge of a 15-year employee in whose locker was found a bottle containing a tiny amount of liquor:

> It is true that the whiskey left in the bottle . . . barely covered the bottom of the bottle and only by tilting it to an angle could one discern the existence of an estimated 1/10th of a very small jigger. . . . It is also true that the contents in its totality would not even bring meager solace to one with a thirst for the intoxicating effects of liquor. Yet these considerations do not detract from the essential fact that intoxicating liquor . . . was found in the grievant's locker. This is enough to constitute a violation of the letter of the company rule, and I dismiss as unworthy of belief the grievant's explanation that he merely put an empty bottle into his locker because he intended to use it as a container for medicine for athlete's feet which he expected to get from the dispensary. The probabilities are that more was in it earlier . . . .
>
> . . .
>
> Naturally one has sympathy for one who has 15 years of service . . . but this is no basis for setting aside the discipline the company has seen fit to impose. This plant which runs hot steel is not a setting in which to temporize with the application of rules relative to alcohol and the threat it poses to the safety of employees. The company has met its burden of proof and it would be improper in this case for the arbitrator to substitute his judgment by imposing a lesser penalty.[19]

An important factor in this case was that on the day the liquor was discovered the grievant suffered a serious accident in the mill while working with a high BAC, circumstances which tended to confirm that there had been more whiskey in the bottle earlier in the day and that he had consumed it. While arbitrators consider a rule against simple possession of alcohol unassailable on grounds of reasonableness, a finding that a grievant not only possessed but drank the alcohol is likely to increase the probability that the discipline will be upheld.

Conversely, a finding that an employee merely possessed alcohol, even in circumstances which strongly suggest that drinking was intended, may not support discharge where the rules clearly distinguish between possession and consumption or being under the influence. An employee whose duties included driving cars was reinstated by an arbitrator because the grievant had poured himself a drink but had not yet drunk it. There was an employer policy against possession or use of alcohol, but the collective bargaining agreement allowed discharge only for a repetition within six months of an offense for which an employee had been warned in writing or suspended. The employer nevertheless discharged the grievant summarily, citing a contract provision dispensing with the warning if the employee is under the influence of alcohol:

> No warning notice or initial hearing need be given in case of . . . being under the influence of narcotics or intoxicating beverages.

The arbitrator concluded:

> It is clear from the plain and unambiguous language . . . that an employee may not be suspended or discharged for *possession* of an intoxicating beverage without a prior *written* warning issued within a six month period; and that summary suspension or discharge may be imposed only if there is evidence of being "under the influence". . . . Simply put: unless there is consumption, an employee cannot be under the influence.
>
> The arbitrator shares the company's concern for the safety and well-being of its employees and the public it serves; and its policy against possession and use of intoxicating beverages and narcotics is commendable. That having been stated, however, the arbitrator cannot, as the company urges, construe the narrow language of [the collective bargaining agreement] in such a way as to implement the company's desired enforcement of its broad policy.[20]

Off-the-Job Drinking

An employer's right to prohibit drinking on business premises is rarely questioned, but a less settled issue is the employer's authority to discipline an employee because of drinking which takes place off the premises and at times when the employee might be regarded as off-duty.

Motor Vehicle Code Infractions

The issue is typically presented when an employee's off-duty use of alcohol leads to a motor vehicle code infraction. Is the employer justified in taking disciplinary action as a result? There is in arbitration a well-established doctrine that an employee's behavior during his off-duty hours is not properly the employer's concern unless the behavior directly impinges upon the employer's business interests. In what is perhaps the *locus classicus,* the doctrine was framed in these terms:

> While it is true that the employer does not [by virtue of the employment relationship] become the guardian of the employee's every personal action and does not exercise parental control, it is equally true that in those areas having to do with the employer's business, the employer has the right to terminate the relationship if the employee's wrongful actions injuriously affect the business.
>
> The connection between the facts which occur and the extent to which the business is affected must be reasonable and discernible. They must be such as could logically be expected to cause some result in the employer's affairs. Each case must be measured on its own merits.[21]

In cases dealing with alcohol, discipline is sometimes imposed on an employee for driving off-duty while intoxicated in a company vehicle. In such cases, the employer's interests are often seen to be directly involved. In one case where the contract permitted discharges without warning for "drinking related to . . . employment," an arbitrator ruled that an employee who drove a company truck on personal business after hours while intoxicated was properly discharged. Noting that the truck was left with the grievant so that he could go out on business errands directly from his home, the arbitrator wrote:

> It could be argued that drinking related to his employment would have to take place on the premises of the employer.
>
> This would have been a reasonable requirement except for the willing or unwilling custody on the part of the grievant of the company vehicle.[22]

In contrast, an employee convicted of drunken driving in a personal automobile and discharged as a result was reinstated by an arbitrator, who ruled:

> At the time of his arrest the grievant was driving his own vehicle, was on his own time and was not engaged in any business of his employer. . . .
>
> . . .
>
> . . . [E]xceptions and extension of the employer's disciplinary rights beyond the immediate employment relationship should be expressly set forth in the contract and may not be

> deemed to exist by implication. The conclusion is required that under the contract language, the right to discipline for intoxication, neglect of work or the violation of "any acceptable *factory* rule" is applicable to an employee's conduct during his hours of work. . . . It does not seem reasonable that the parties intended that a "factory" rule should extend so as to govern acts of intoxication while within the privacy of the employee's home.[23]

In another case a few years later, however, an arbitrator upheld the discharge of an employee for having been convicted of driving a motor vehicle while under the influence of alcohol. The company rules dealing with alcohol did not mention off-duty drinking, but the arbitrator relied upon a rule which listed "violation of criminal law" as one of the offenses that may lead to dismissal:

> [T]he factor which is most important in this case is that a company rule was violated by the grievant's conviction. This rule states nothing about conduct on or off the premises but merely says "violation of criminal law" may be grounds for dismissal. The grievant's conduct came under this rule and the rule could be applied by the company unless it was unreasonable. The mere fact that the rule was general and applied to conduct on and off the premises would not of itself make it unreasonable.[24]

It is worth noting the union's argument in this case that the discipline policy was inconsistent because in several other instances employees convicted of similar infractions had not been discharged. The employer freely acknowledged its omissions in the past but attributed the discrepancy partly to the circumstance that some convictions came to the company's notice and some did not. It might, of course, be argued with equal force that an employer's inherently imperfect knowledge of employees' off-premises activities is a good reason for not attempting to impose discipline for behavior unrelated to the workplace.

Infractions Clearly Affecting the Employer

Certainly, disciplinary action for off-duty drinking is easier to sustain where the employer rules encompass only infractions which clearly affect the company's operations or reputation. An arbitrator upheld the discharge of an employee on a temporary assignment away from his home plant who was involved in two serious automobile accidents within a few days. Each time he was off-duty but driving a car that his company had authorized him to rent. In both instances, the state police reported that the grievant had been driving at an excessive speed and that his breath smelled of alcohol. In one of the accidents, a fellow employee was severely injured.

The arbitrator noted that the employer had posted a rule prohibiting conduct "adversely affecting the interests or reputation of the company." This prohibition applied to conduct "on company property and elsewhere." The arbitrator held:

> The union is . . . correct when it asserts, as a general rule, that the company has no right to regulate or control the private lives of its employees. However, this general rule is subject to an exception. Where the off-the-job conduct of an employee adversely affects the interests or reputation of the company, such conduct may properly be prohibited.
>
> In the case of [the grievant], substantial evidence was produced by the company demonstrating that notoriety resulted from the two accidents. Publicity such as this is particularly damaging to a company attempting to establish a harmonious relationship within a rural area where it is the largest single employer. There is no doubt in the mind of the arbitrator that the company has a justifiable right in protecting itself against such damage to its reputation.
>
> . . .
>
> It may well be true that the company has no prohibition against employees drinking on their own time. Nevertheless, all employees of the company, if they intend to indulge themselves in this manner, must do so under circumstances that will not harm the reputation of the company.[25]

Similarly, an arbitrator upheld the discharge of an airline clerk who, when scheduled to go on duty, awoke in a police station after a drinking bout. The incident, noted the arbitrator, involved more than just a failure to call in to report an impending absence; the grievant had "conspicuously flaunted his inebriation in public and made it a matter of public record." The arbitrator wrote:

> The image presented by the grievant's "sleeping it off" in the jail is not reassuring to persons who know that he works for a particular employer charged with exercising a high degree of care at all times. Gossip flows about a station house and jail, and more often than not the exact relationship of a particular employee to the operation of a carrier is not known or recognized. There are types of employment where this might not make much difference, but grievant did not associate himself with such. The minister who curses, the lawyer who violates the law, the doctor who breaks the health rules he prescribes for patients, and all

> sorts of individuals who by their conduct besmirch their vocational callings have an added burden of maintaining appearances and reputations.[26]

In a related case, the arrest of a grievant on a charge of public drunkenness while off-duty was the immediate cause for a discharge grounded upon his overall record of poor performance and excessive absenteeism. In upholding the discharge, the arbitrator observed:

> It is commonly known that drinking . . . leads to carelessness and other well known difficulties and complications. The employer should be free to protect the safety of and maintain good morale of its other employees and its property by discharging any employee when it has good reason to believe that his drinking habits contribute to his absenteeism, his work performance and his relationship to his fellow employees. . . . Intemperance in the use of liquor to the extent that it makes a worker unsteady on his job is never condoned by the union or industry.[27]

Drinking During Meal Periods

There is an even more direct bearing on the workplace when the off-duty involvement with alcohol occurs during meal periods, since the employee's performance for the remainder of the shift may be affected. An employer's authority to prohibit drinking during lunch, even off the premises, was upheld by an arbitrator, who found that the union had given the employer to understand that it shared management's concern about the consequences of consuming alcohol on breaks.

The employer posted an amendment to the company rules that prohibited not only on-premises drinking but "drinking of alcoholic beverages during lunch or dinner period during working hours, on or off plant premises." An employee spotted by supervisors drinking beer at a nearby cafe during his break was discharged under this rule. The union objected that the disciplinary provisions of the contract did not authorize the company to adopt the rule amendment and that it was "standard doctrine that the company cannot discipline an employee for off-premise drinking without showing that the employee was unfit for work when he returned." The arbitrator, who sustained the discharge, answered the union objection as follows:

> For some time the company had been having problems due to men drinking during their mealtime break. This was most seri-

ous in the maintenance division because of dangers to the men involved and [to] others working with them, and especially on the swing and night shifts, when the men work without normal supervision. The matter had been discussed with the union shop committee and with the safety committee, and it is conceded that union officials "suggested it be checked into."

. . .

. . . [The union] led the company to believe that it saw an evil in lunch hour drinking that should be stopped. Management was fully justified in concluding that this was a joint endeavor. . . .

. . . If it was not a proper interpretation of a mutual understanding of the contract, the union should have made this clear long ago.[28]

A similar result was reached in a case involving a municipal employer whose rules prohibited "drinking during working hours." The grievant had been observed drinking beer while on an unpaid lunch break at a tavern, outside which he had parked the city-owned vehicle that he drove, a truck-mounted crane. He was suspended for one day without pay. In upholding the suspension, the arbitrator noted:

The union takes the position that the employee was on his own time, and is, therefore, free to do whatever he sees fit, and can not be disciplined for conduct engaged in during his non-paid lunch period.

. . .

. . . It is not claimed that [the grievant] was finished working for the day. He was, in fact, on his way to another job where his crane was needed to lift a piece of fallen concrete. [He] was, therefore, still employed by the city, and not in the same position as though he had not yet reported for work for the day or completely finished with work and on his own time until again reporting for work on a succeeding shift.

. . .

The employee is still in possession of the city's equipment and still charged with its safe operation.[29]

Special Requirements for Past Alcohol Abusers

An employee's off-duty drinking may be perceived as a particularly serious threat to the employer if he has been disciplined for using alcohol to excess in the past and seems to be lapsing into his former pattern of abuse. When an employee is seen violating a pledge of total abstinence, albeit during his off hours, the employer may conclude that he has resumed uncontrolled drinking. That is especially true if the pledge is made as part of a "last chance" reinstatement agreement (see "'Last Chance' Agreements" in Chapter 8). The employer then can insist that the agreement expressly authorizes an extension of its disciplinary rights to the off-duty sphere.

These arguments were presented when an alcoholic employee was discharged for violating an employer rule against possession of alcoholic beverages on the premises—and then reinstated under quite specific conditions. The conditions, to which he agreed, were as follows:

> 1. He would not consume alcoholic beverages from that point on, anywhere, at any time.
> 2. He would continue his counseling sessions with [his parish priest].
> 3. He would continue to attend regular meetings of [Alcoholics Anonymous].
> 4. He would not go to Schuster's [an eating place with a bar] for lunch, or [for] any other purpose, so that he would not be tempted to drink.

About five months after his reinstatement, a supervisor encountered the grievant in Schuster's during his lunch break, sitting at the bar with a glass of beer in front of him. He was discharged. Grieving the discharge, the union contended that he had been denied "equal justice," and at the end of the hearing, the arbitrator recorded, the grievant remarked that "he couldn't understand why a requirement had been placed on him that had not been placed on any other employee of the company."

The arbitrator, finding no evidence that the first discharge was unjustified, concluded that the company had a right to attach to his reinstatement the four conditions, which, he held, were not burdensome:

> Ordinarily management does not reserve a right to supervise an employee's personal life away from the plant, but where as here a condition has been placed on an employee's reinstatement to avoid a certain place because of his weakness . . . and the hazardous condition of his employment, then such condition is valid.

The arbitrator concluded that the grievant had violated the terms of the reinstatement agreement, and he upheld the discharge, observing:

> Management had gone out of its way to reinstate him. [The grievant] created his own problem.[30]

Drinking While "Subject to Duty"

Drinking may be explicitly barred during off-duty periods in which employees are likely to be summoned to work at any moment. The railroad industry regulation known as "Rule G" prohibits the use of alcoholic beverages by employees while "subject to duty" as well as while working. The scope of this phrase has been tested in a number of cases.

In one, the grievant had been arrested by the police on a charge of driving while intoxicated. At the time he was supposed to be on-call he was in jail, causing him to miss a telephoned summons to report for duty. As a result, he was discharged for violating Rule G. In sustaining the discharge, the Public Law Board concluded:

> The record establishes beyond cavil that [the grievant] was culpable of unmitigated serious misconduct which, more often than not, is considered terminal behavior in the railroad industry.[31]

In another case, the grievant, an engineer, had pleaded guilty to a charge of being intoxicated after an altercation at a campsite where he was fishing. The grievant's next regular duty was two days away. The incident did not come to the carrier's attention until a security officer discovered the record of conviction about a month later. The employee was then discharged. The Public Law Board which heard the case concluded:

> [The grievant] was on a rotating pool assignment with a fixed pattern of service. There was no reasonable expectation that his regular turn would be called for service on . . . the day of the alleged violation. While he could have been called for emergency duty we think . . . that Rule G's reference to "subject to duty" does not contemplate emergency duty.

The grievant's reinstatement was without pay, however, because he was found to have violated another rule prohibiting conduct that is "quarrelsome or otherwise vicious" or causes the employer a "loss of good will."[32]

In a third railroad case, a brakeman with 17 years of service grieved his discharge, which had been imposed under Rule G and other regulations, for becoming intoxicated and firing a rifle several times in the town that was his away-from-home terminal. He had been off-duty since the previous evening and was awaiting his turn to work. The Public Law Board held:

> Although the incidents took place off carrier's property and outside working hours, he was subject to call and therefore in violation of Rule G's prohibition. . . .
>
> Accordingly . . . the record does provide a sound basis for discipline. Dismissal, on the other hand, is excessive. [The grievant's] drinking was confined to his own room away from carrier's premises. While he was subject to call, there is no evidence that he was called. . . .
>
> In the light of this record, we will direct carrier to offer claimant immediate reinstatement, with seniority rights unimpaired, but without back pay.[33]

Rules on Possession, Use and Sale of Drugs

Employer rules against possession of intoxicants other than alcohol frequently fail to define the substances prohibited, an omission which may lead to differing interpretations. Banning "drugs" raises the question of whether prescription drugs are also included (when abused or used without prescription) or whether only those drugs whose possession is illegal under state and federal law come within the purview of the rule. Employing the broad term "narcotics"—a pharmacological category which embraces primarily heroin, morphine or other opium derivatives—invites disputes when the employee is involved with a substance which acts as a stimulant or a hallucinogen. Moreover, a substance such as methadone (see "Rehabilitating Drug Abusers" in Chapter 2), which is technically a narcotic, can serve rehabilitative purposes, a situation which the framers of the employer rule may not have envisioned. It is, therefore, crucial to frame a rule in terms that are both comprehensive and specific and which make appropriate distinctions between alcohol and drugs, and among various types of drugs.

Under rules which prohibit possession of "narcotics" at the workplace, arbitrators have seen no difficulty in sustaining at least some discipline against employees who were involved with marijuana[34] and Valium.[35] Relying upon a requirement that "conduct must conform to accepted standards of decency and morality, as well as laws that are enacted," an employer suspended for six months an employee who was arrested for marijuana possession; an arbitrator voided the discipline because the arrest was off the premises.[36] Some misimpressions about the intended scope of a rule against unauthorized possession of drugs might be avoided by casting it in terms of "controlled substances," since that is a category broad enough to encompass both narcotic and non-narcotic drugs, including prescription drugs, whose possession is regulated by law.

Interpreting the Terminology

In a case in which the employer rules prohibited employees from "[d]rinking or being under the influence of drugs or alcohol while on company premises," an arbitrator rejected the union's argument that it was improper to discipline a grievant who was incapacitated at work by the effects of legal drugs prescribed for him by a doctor. The grievant was taking a variety of prescription drugs, including the barbiturate Phenobarbital, tranquilizers and anti-epileptic medicines. He had a history of both drug abuse and alcoholism and had been involved in 11 industrial accidents in less than three years. He was disciplined after being found in a daze while working near vats of acid. Upholding the penalty, the arbitrator wrote:

> The prohibition is clearly designed with a two-fold purpose. First and foremost, it is a safety rule to protect both the employee who might be under the influence of drugs and his fellow employees from harm or injury. Secondly, it is designed to protect the company against paying wages to an employee who is incapable of performing productively with reasonable efficiency. Given these two clear purposes of the rule, it is immaterial whether the drug is prescriptive and its possession is legal or illegal. . . . The prohibition against being under the influence of alcohol is not limited nor should a reasonable employee understand it to be limited to illegal alcohol such as untaxed bootleg. Neither should an employee understand the prohibition against being under the influence of drugs to be limited to illegal drugs. The clear purposes . . . intended by the rule are just as applicable to an employee under the influence of legal drugs as to an employee under the influence of illegal drugs.[37]

An employer rule against possession of "habit-forming drugs" has been held to apply to marijuana by an arbitrator, although he disallowed the full penalty because it was doubtful the grievant had possessed enough to cause impairment. The marijuana had been found by the police, who searched the grievant at the plant; he later pleaded guilty to a criminal charge of possession. The arbitrator rejected the union's argument that the grievant did not intend to use the marijuana, but he held:

> There was no reliable evidence that might establish that even if he had been able to use the drugs . . . there was a sufficient quantity . . . to cause any impairment which would have been sufficient to adversely affect his work performance.

The arbitrator reinstated the grievant without awarding back pay

> since to do so would lead to the misconception that I condone the [grievant's] possession of marijuana on company premises.[38]

The Employee's Intent

An employee's intent with respect to the drugs may be as significant as the nature of the drugs themselves, particularly since "street drugs" often are not what they appear to be (see "Substance Identification" in Chapter 6). Some pills sold illicitly are manufactured in bootleg laboratories to mimic the size, shape and color of standard-brand products, although the contents might bear little similarity to the original. May an employee be disciplined for selling what is ostensibly a controlled substance, even if it is not?

A shipyard laborer with substantial seniority was discharged for violating an employer rule against possessing a controlled substance on company property. He had been arrested by the police while in possession of a bag of 600 double-scored white pills which the police believed to be amphetamines but which tests later showed to be a non-controlled substance. The employer, nevertheless, urged the arbitrator to sustain the discharge on the ground that the grievant was selling the pills to fellow employees *as* a controlled substance, an activity which it said constituted a violation of state law and a form of "theft through misrepresentation." The arbitrator concluded:

> No one saw [the grievant] make a sale of the pills holding them out to be a controlled substance. The pills were in fact not a controlled substance and therefore mere possession of the pills is not a crime nor is it against any company rule.

Although the employer thus lacked just cause for the discharge, the grievant was not entitled to back pay:

> During the two months that he sold pills he made approximately 24 sales for each bag of pills he purchased and he purchased one or two bags each week. He thus devoted a substantial number of hours of working time to this private enterprise as well as absorbing an equivalent amount of working time from his customers.
>
> . . . The grievant's conduct was dangerously unwise and reasonably falls within the company rule against neglect of duty. . . . The company should not be penalized for specifying the wrong offense and the grievant, whose conduct was thoroughly reprehensible, should not be rewarded for establishing by his own admission that he violated company rules.[39]

Intent was also the issue in a case in which an employee was suspended for one day for leaving the workplace without permission after apparently beginning to feel the effects of eating a brownie laced with marijuana. The employer's rules prohibited employees from being under the influence of "narcotics or other mind-altering drugs" and provided for disciplinary suspension without a prior warning in cases of "willful or negligent misconduct of a serious nature." The arbitrator found that the grievant had innocently eaten the brownie, which had been offered to him by a fellow worker, and that neither person knew the brownie contained marijuana. (It had been baked by the girlfriend of the co-worker's roommate.) The arbitrator ordered the grievant made whole for the suspension, ruling that, given

> [t]here is no evidence that he was responsible for his illness or that he voluntarily came under the influence of drugs or [a] "mind altering substance," I find that his departure was not for "willful or negligent misconduct of a serious nature" . . . .
>
> . . . [W]here the employee panics and leaves work with the stressful condition of not knowing what effect a drug unknowingly taken would have upon him—such circumstances do not make the offense "serious" . . . .[40]

Possession of Drugs

Arbitrators have also read an intent requirement into employer rules against simple possession of drugs. An airline flight attendant, to take one example, was discharged for violating a company rule which prohibited "possession of . . . illegal or dangerous drugs on company premises or while in uniform."

There was no question that the flight attendant was in uniform and on company premises when marijuana was discovered in a portfolio she was carrying. The grievant said she did not know how the drugs got into the portfolio. The arbitrator held:

> [T]o establish a violation of the company rule it is not enough to prove mere possession of the drug. The company must also show that grievant had knowledge of the possession. The rule prohibits illegal possession. Under [state] law possession is not illegal per se. The possession must be [knowing or intentional]. . . .
>
> . . .
>
> . . . I have a reasonable doubt that grievant knew the marijuana was in her possession. There is no direct evidence that she had such knowledge. . . . The company has emphasized that grievant was unable to offer any explanation as to how the drug got in her possession [,] implying that the burden is upon her to do so. But this is not correct. She is not required to prove her innocence.[41]

Here again one notes the tendency to assimilate criminal standards to labor arbitration in cases involving illegal drugs (see "Quantum of Proof in Alcohol and Drug Cases" in Chapter 4). In striking contrast, few arbitrators seem to demand proof that an employee's possession of a bottle of liquor was knowing or intentional.

Employment Forms and the Drug Abuser

Some employers seek to screen employees by means of medical questionnaires and tests designed to detect drug abusers. Employers may require a medical form to be filled out when applying for reassignment to a different job, and they sometimes ask employees to submit to a urine test for the presence of drugs.

Disciplinary action taken on the basis of such screening procedures has come under arbitral scrutiny. In one case, an employee of a construction firm, applying for a crane operator's position, filled out a medical form on which Question 11 asked: "Are you taking any type of medication at present (insulin, tranquilizers, etc.)?" The employee answered negatively, but a laboratory analysis of his urine sample, taken the same day, revealed traces of amphetamines. The company discharged him for "falsification of signed medical forms." The arbitrator ruled that the discharge was not for just cause because of the ambiguity of the word "medication." He wrote:

> The layman understands that concept to mean a medicine used to cure or heal, to relieve pain, or to control a disease. The two illustrative examples in the question, significantly, are of drugs regularly taken—probably on a daily basis. If [the grievant] is an occasional "pill popper" (and there is no evidence here to prove or disprove that hypothesis), he could truthfully have answered Question 11 in the negative. . . .
>
> . . . It is significant that [the grievant] was not fired for using drugs, or for being under the influence of drugs, or for poor workmanship, or for carelessness, or for poor attendance. The company carefully chose, as its ground for termination, the alleged incorrect statement. . . . It would be unfair, however, to discharge an employee on such ground unless the question itself were clear and unambiguous and susceptible of only one interpretation. That is particularly important when the answer called for is either yes or no. Questions such as—Specify the drugs, if any, which you have taken during the past X days. Explain the reason, quantity (or dosage) and purpose—might elicit more informative answers.
>
> . . .
>
> Does [management] intend that the "occasional" user be barred from employment or from assignments to particularly hazardous jobs? If so, there should be a clear statement of such rule. . . . (The union, of course, has a right to grieve about the reasonableness of any rule.) The employees would then know where they stand. But the "Medical History" approach used here does not appear to meet the problem squarely or to make clear to employees what the rules are or what conduct is expected.[42]

Refusal to Answer

May an employee refuse with impunity to answer an employer's question about his current use of drugs? That issue was presented when an employee of a drug manufacturing company underwent "re-evaluation" by the firm after being convicted of a felony. He was asked to fill out a screening form on which appeared the following question:

> In the past three years, have you ever knowingly used any narcotics, amphetamines or barbiturates, or any other controlled substances, other than those prescribed for you by a physician?

The employee declined to answer that question. The employer subsequently discharged him, a penalty based partly on his failure to respond. Although the discharge was upheld on other grounds, the arbitrator ruled that the failure to answer, by itself, would not have merited such a severe penalty. The arbitrator acknowledged that

> the company . . . makes products much sought after by criminal elements, and there is an almost daily effort required . . . to keep its products from those who would misuse them.
>
> . . .
>
> . . . The employer has a right to determine if an employee may try to use its drugs himself, or if his access to drugs may be dangerous to himself or his employer. So that seeking such information . . . is not an invasion of privacy.

Nevertheless, the arbitrator concluded, requiring an employee to answer the question might be tantamount to compulsory self-incrimination:

> That being the case, an employee could refuse to answer such a question on the grounds that the answer might tend to incriminate him. However, this is not to say that the company does not have the right to ask the question. It may. But it must take whatever answer is given—even a plea that the answer might be self-incriminating.

Since the grievant gave no answer,

> the company was within its rights in imposing discipline of some nature. Standing alone, however, such refusal to answer would not justify discharge.[43]

Employment Applications

Another form of screening is the employment application questionnaire which asks whether the applicant has been convicted of a crime. Persons whose involvement with drugs has led to a criminal conviction may be held accountable for misstatements about the incident, even though it was long in the past. An employee who answered "no" to the question "Have you ever been arrested or convicted of any crime?" was held properly discharged later when a conviction for selling marijuana came to the employer's attention. The arbitrator noted:

> He . . . worked for 11 months for the employer. There was never any indication that he was peddling marijuana, selling it on the premises, involving his employment with marijuana. That was in his past.
>
> . . .
>
> [But] it is the opinion of the arbitrator that falsification of application for employment was a dishonest act and especially so when it was done willfully and knowingly.[44]

Rule G: A Case Study

In the railroad industry, the regulation known as Rule G, discussed previously in connection with off-duty drinking (see "Off-the-Job Drinking" in this chapter), offers an example of a punitive rule, which has been supplemented by a policy of permitting alcoholics and drug abusers an opportunity to rehabilitate themselves. Rule G reads as follows:

> The use of alcoholic beverages or narcotics by employees subject to duty is prohibited. Being under the influence of alcoholic beverages or narcotics while on duty or on company property is prohibited. The use or possession of alcoholic beverages while on duty or on company property is prohibited.[45]

A single infraction of Rule G has often been held to be grounds for dismissal of an employee. Some carriers, however, operate Employee Assistance Programs through which discharged Rule G violators may secure reinstatement. The Burlington Northern Railroad, for example, has issued a policy statement which stipulates:

> Under a Rule G dismissal a minimum of four months must pass before a request for reinstatement will be considered. Reinstatement will at no time be automatic and employees dismissed under Rule G will not be reinstated at any time unless they have contacted and cooperated with the Employee Assistance Program.[46]

The policy figured in the case of an employee who was discharged after being discovered drinking in a bar while still on duty. A Public Law Board determined that the employee was guilty of a Rule G infraction but awarded as follows:

> The [railroad] . . . has offered to reinstate [the grievant] conditioned on successful participation in the . . . Employee Assistance Program. Despite the fact that the record shows that [he] has declined participation, that remedy will be reoffered by this board, providing [the grievant] makes known . . . his acceptance of this offer within thirty . . . days of this award.[47]

An employee who re-offends against Rule G is not offered a further opportunity for reinstatement. That aspect of the policy was challenged by a trainman who was dismissed for violating Rule G a second time. A Public Law Board accepted the railroad's finding that the grievant was "under the influence of alcohol *while on duty* and within minutes of active work on a train." The union had argued that considerable time had elapsed since the last Rule G offense and that the grievant had been making efforts at rehabilitation. However, the board concluded, in effect, that since the policy of offering reinstatement for a first offense was discretionary, the carrier's refusal to reinstate after a second was also discretionary. The board noted that the reinstatement policy was promulgated on a "leniency basis" and that the carrier had a "uniform policy *not* to grant such leniency in the case of a second Rule G offense."[48]

8

Alcohol and Drugs in the Collective Bargaining Agreement

Contractual Disciplinary Clauses

On the whole, collective bargaining agreements have tended to be silent on the subject of alcoholism or drug abuse among employees, leaving the field to unilaterally promulgated employer rules. A survey of 500 agreements collected by the Federal Bureau of Labor Statistics revealed that only 29 (six percent) contained clauses specifically dealing with employee alcohol use. All of these clauses, which are summarized in Table 3 (see page 128), deal with discipline for alcohol-related infractions; none makes provision for the treatment of employees suffering from alcoholism.[1]

Incorporating alcohol and drug rules in the agreement offers advantages for both parties. Disputes that may arise later are likely to involve only the application of the rule in individual cases rather than the inherent reasonableness of the rule. Incorporation in the agreement also preempts the issue of whether employees have been duly notified of the rule's existence. Mutually agreed-upon rules, furthermore, allow the parties to jointly make critical choices of emphasis, both in defining the offenses and in laying down a disciplinary procedure.

Contract Variations

Definitions of offenses vary considerably. The specific offenses covered by the contracts in Table 3 were variously

Table 3. Inventory of contract language on alcohol in contracts covering 1,000 or more workers in 1973

Company	Unions	Contract Provision on Alcoholism
Pet Milk Corp.	International Brotherhood of Teamsters, Locals 22, 23, 28, 61, 71, 322, 391, 509, 592, 822	Immediate discharge for drinking, under the influence.
Associated Producers & Packers	IBT, Locals 231, 252, 599, 788	Immediate discharge for intoxicated on the job
New England Bakers	IBT	Immediate discharge for drunkenness
Dairy Industry Industrial Relations Association (Los Angeles) Master Agreement	IBT, Locals 92, 166, 186, 572, 683, 871, 898, 952, 982	Immediate discharge for drinking on the job
Ice Cream Council (Chicago)	IBT, Local 717	Discharge for "proven drinking or proven drunkenness while on duty or proven under influence or possession of illegal drugs while on duty"
Seabrook Farms Co., Inc. (Bridgeport, NJ)	Amalgamated Food; Aluminum Workers Union, Local 56	Immediate discharge for use or possession of intoxicating beverages
Lumber & Mill Employers Assoc.	Millmen, Locals 42, 262, 550, 2095	Discharge or suspension for intoxication or impairment resulting from consumption of alcohol or drugs
Soft Drink Bottlers (Chicago)	IBT, Local 744	Immediate discharge for drunkenness, drinking alcoholic beverages while at work or unlawful use or possession of drugs or narcotics while at work
Consolidated Papers, Inc. Consoweid Corp. (WI)	Paperworkers, Locals 187, 116, 359, 94, 306, 81, 1985, 102; International Brotherhood of Electrical Workers, Local 1147	Immediate discharge for being under the influence of an intoxicating beverage

Contd. on next page

Table 3.—*Contd.*

Company	Unions	Contract Provision on Alcoholism
Brown Co.	International Brotherhood of Pulp, Sulphite and Paper Mill Workers, Local 78	Warning, reprimand and discharge for (*1*) reporting under the influence of liquor, (*2*) drinking or possession of alcoholic beverages on company property
Nekoosa Edwards	Paperworkers, Locals 59, 52; Machinists, Local 1543; Plumbers, Local 807; Electricians, Local 1786	Discipline or discharge for being intoxicated, or having narcotics, dangerous drugs on company property or reporting to work under the influence of liquor, narcotics or dangerous drugs provided that such prohibition shall not include drugs taken according to the prescription of a licensed physician
Great Northern Paper Co.	Papermakers, Locals 27, 37; Pulp, Sulphite and Paper, Local 12; Plumbers and Pipefitters, Local 485; IBEW, Local 471; Firemen and Oilers, Locals 69, 261, 362; Machinists, Local 156; Carpenters, Locals 685, 1612	Immediate discharge for bringing intoxicating beverages onto the premises
Thilmany Pulp & Paper Co.	Paperworkers, Locals 20, 147	"Discharge for just and proper cause . . . including alcoholism"
Westvaco Corp. (VA, MD, PA Mills)	United Paperworkers International Union, Locals 675, 676, 677	Discharge for "(*b*) Bringing or having intoxicants in the mill; (*c*) Reporting for duty so under the influence of liquor as not to be capable of performing his duties"
Bowaters Southern Paper Corp.	UPWIU, Locals 788, 789, 790, 653; IBEW, Local 175	Discipline or discharge for bringing intoxicants into mill and reporting under the influence of intoxicants or narcotics

Contd. on next page

Table 3.—*Contd.*

Company	Unions	Contract Provision on Alcoholism
Inland Container Corp.	UPWIU, Locals 31, 114, 1046, 993, 4658, 737, 954, 828	Discipline for bringing intoxicants into plant, consuming intoxicants in plant or on premises, reporting under the influence of alcoholic beverages causing interference with productive efficiency
Fisher Controls Co. (IA)	International Union of United Automobile, Aerospace and Agricultural Implement Workers of America, Local 893	Disciplinary action for reporting under the influence of intoxicants or narcotics or consuming same during work day or bringing onto premises
Midwest Manufacturing Corp. (Galesburg, IL)	International Association of Machinists and Aerospace Workers, Local 2063	Prohibited: Intoxicants on duty or under the influence, using or possessing—First offense: 30 days' suspension. Second offense: discharge
Greyhound Corp.	Council of Western Greyhound, Amalgamated Division and the Amalgamated Transit Unions covering Divisions 1055, 1222, 1223, 1225, 1384, 1471, 1508	Discharge for intoxication or use of drugs
Household Goods Moving & Storage	IBT, Locals 186, 235, 389, 467, 542, 692, 871	Discharge for drunkenness or drinking on the job
United Parcel Service	IBT, Local 542	Immediate discharge; no notice to union; use on job, reporting under the influence
Western States Area Office Employers, Employed by Private, Common and Contract Carriers	IBT	Discharge without notice for drunkenness
Western States Area Automotive Shop and Truck Services	IBT	Immediate discharge for drunkenness

Contd. on next page

Table 3.—*Cont'd.*

Company	Unions	Contract Provision on Alcoholism
Merchant Fast Motor Lines, Inc.	Union of Transportation Employees, Local 102870	Discharge without warning for drinking or being under the influence of intoxicating beverages or for possession on duty or on property
Savannah Maritime Assoc.	Longshoremen's Association, Local 1414	Discipline or discharge; intoxication prohibited
General Contractors Assoc. in New York	Laborers International Union of North America, Local 737	Immediate dismissal for use of intoxicants or illegal drugs
Employing Metallic Furring and Lathing Assoc. of NY	Wood, Wire and Metal Lathers International Union, Local 46	Alcoholic beverages not permitted on job
Retail Maintenance Resilient Floor Coverers Agreement, Dockbuilders Agreement, Outside Building Construction Agreement	Carpenters District Council of NY, Local 1456	Immediate dismissal; consumption of alcohol on the job site
Association of General Contractors of America (West Coast Florida)	LIUNA, Locals 512, 1207, 1240	Discipline and discharge; no drinking

Source: C. J. Schramm, *Development of Comprehensive Language on Alcoholism in Collective Bargaining Agreements,* 38 JOURNAL OF STUDIES ON ALCOHOL 1409—11. Reprinted by permission.

defined as shown in the list below.

- drinking on the job;
- drunkenness;
- impairment resulting from consumption of alcohol;
- reporting under the influence;
- bringing intoxicants into the plant;
- use or possession of intoxicating beverages at work.

The disciplinary procedure also varies considerably. A striking feature of the Table 3 clauses, the survey found, is that they tend to divide almost evenly into two categories: those which provide for immediate discharge for the first alcohol-related offense and those which provide for progressive discipline, including warnings and suspensions, before a discharge is imposed.[2] Moreover, among contracts generally, there are strong differences about which offenses are specified as the more serious. In some, possession of alcohol is treated as a graver offense than being under the influence of alcohol; in others, being under the influence is treated more harshly than possessing alcohol in the plant.

The former type of provision, to take one illustration, figured in a case in which the union argued that the grievant had been charged with the wrong offense. The grievant had been discharged for possession of alcohol. The contract provided for discharge for "good cause," which was defined as including "violation by an employee of any published reasonable rule of the company." For several years preceding the case, an agreement had been in effect between the union and company which recognized the company's policy on intoxicants and narcotics as a "published reasonable rule." The policy provided, in part:

> For the first offense, any employee, while on company property, who has intoxicants or narcotics in his possession, in his locker or in any other location, will be discharged.
>
> Any employee under the influence of intoxicants or narcotics, while on company property, will be penalized as follows:
>
> 1. For the first offense in any five-year period, the employee will be suspended for five scheduled workdays.
> 2. For the second offense in any five-year period, the employee will be suspended for ten scheduled workdays.
> 3. For the third offense in any five-year period, the employee will be discharged.[3]

During the arbitration, the union refrained from challenging the reasonableness of the possession rule; rather, it took the position—unsuccessfully—that the grievant's true offense was to have violated the rule against being under the influence, which would have resulted in a penalty less severe than discharge.[4]

Quite the opposite sort of contractual arrangement formed the basis of another alcohol case, involving the employee of a car rental firm. It called for warnings and suspensions before discharge for possession of intoxicants and most other offenses:

> The employer shall not discipline nor suspend any employee without just cause. He shall give at least one written warning

> notice to an employee before he is discharged or suspended for a repetition of the same complaint. Such written notice shall expire after six (6) months and will not be used as evidence in the grievance procedure.

But another provision offered a broad exemption from the warning requirements in certain matters:

> No warning notice or initial hearing need be given in case of . . . being under the influence of narcotics or intoxicating beverages.[5]

The effect was to allow summary discharge for being under the influence of alcohol but to require progressive discipline for possession. Since the grievant had been seen *with* a cup of liquor but had not been seen to *drink* from it, the arbitrator disallowed the discharge.

Providing for Rehabilitation

From the point of view of arbitration, the framing of bilateral provisions on alcohol and drug offenses should be encouraged, since such provisions help narrow the focus of disputes to factual issues instead of raising the broader issue of the validity of the rules. Given the importance of the subject to the productivity and safety of the workplace, both parties would seem to have an important stake in promulgating a bilateral arrangement. At the same time, however, the parties might consider whether it would not be equally wise to frame a provision for rehabilitation of alcoholics and drug abusers as well as for punishment of infractions.

The reasons for the relative paucity of such provisions in collective bargaining agreements have been catalogued by Professor Carl J. Schramm of the Johns Hopkins University School of Hygiene and Public Health, an authority on labor–management alcoholism programs:

> This has proved to be an area of delicate balance in labor relations. On the one hand, unions have claimed that alcoholism has often served as an excuse to terminate employees whom management found unsatisfactory for other reasons. On the other hand, where contract language existed which provided for medical treatment of alcoholism and a "second chance" before discharge or termination, managements have reported union abuse, claiming that unions often insist on the protection provided for alcoholic employees for workers who are not actually alcoholics.[6]

Several basic elements are needed to produce agreement on this issue, Schramm has concluded:

> Management must conclude that it will gain more by the presence of contract language (a healthier, more contented and productive work force) than it will lose by having traditional management rights limited by contractually binding language. . . . Union leadership must assure the membership that its welfare will be maximized by specific language guaranteeing job rights and a formal discipline and discharge process to any worker identified as being alcoholic.[7]

Examples of Contract Clauses

A number of employers, both public and private, have succeeded in arriving at a mutually-agreed rehabilitation clause. Typically such a clause affords employees some degree of protection from the disciplinary procedure as long as they cooperate in rehabilitation efforts. And the clause may provide for a joint union–management committee to oversee treatment, counseling and referral practices. The following are examples of such contract language:

> The employer and the unions express strong support for programs of self-help. The parties will meet at the national level at least once every six months to discuss existing and new programs. This program of labor–management cooperation shall . . . expand its coverage and consider implementing a pilot project regarding the use of non-hard-core drugs.
>
> An employee's voluntary participation in such programs will be considered favorably in disciplinary proceedings.

* * * * *

> [The state] will introduce procedures under which an employee with a drinking problem is offered rehabilitative assistance before charges are preferred. If the employee refuses to avail himself or herself of assistance and the abuse of alcohol impairs work performance, attendance, conduct or reliability, regular disciplinary procedures for dealing with problem employees will be used.

* * * * *

> [A joint alcoholism committee will] help the employee understand that he may consult on a confidential basis with the plant medical director, or an outside qualified facility or agency,

concerning his alcoholism tendencies without fear of disciplinary action based on such discussion.

* * * * *

[The city] shall designate and train employees as counseling referral officers among the several departments and agencies. Officers shall consider affected employees' counseling needs and refer those employees with problems such as alcoholism . . . to the appropriate agencies and/or resources for proper counseling and treatment. The union shall assist in the administration of this program. Employees designated as counseling referral officers shall be trained and shall assume the aforesaid duties in the course of their employment.[8]

Interpreting a Rehabilitation Clause

How does mutually agreed contract language about the rehabilitation of alcoholics or drug abusers affect the outcome of discipline and discharge arbitrations? A good example is the line of decisions which interpret Section 14-F of the agreement between the United States Steel Corporation and the United Steelworkers of America. The section provides:

> Alcoholism and drug abuse are recognized by the parties to be treatable conditions. Without detracting from the existing rights and obligations of the parties recognized in the other provisions of this agreement, the company and the union agree to cooperate at the plant level in encouraging employees afflicted with alcoholism or drug abuse to undergo a coordinated program directed to the objective of their rehabilitation.

The key question is the extent to which Section 14-F modifies the normal mode of imposing discipline and discharge.

Degree of Causal Connection

A primary factor in the decisions of the parties' Board of Arbitration is the degree of causal connection between the alcoholism or drug abuse and the specific incident for which discipline was invoked. In one case, the grievant was a laborer with less than two years at the plant, during which time he had accumulated six disciplinary actions, including a five-day suspension for absenteeism and failure to report absences properly. He was discharged for the seventh offense.

The grievant testified that at the time of his discharge and during the four previous years he had been drinking a case of beer a day and that he had twice entered detoxification and rehabilitation programs, evidently without success. The arbitrator wrote:

> [T]he union contends that grievant was improperly discharged because he was denied his rights under Section 14-F of the agreement. The union insists that grievant is an alcoholic and, as such, is entitled to a rehabilitation program without regard to the fact that the company was unaware of the grievant's affliction until step 3 of the grievance procedure. It asserts, in essence, that the company failed to fulfill its obligation to ascertain whether grievant's conduct was alcohol-related and, thereafter, failed to afford him a coordinated alcohol rehabilitation program.
>
> The company maintains that grievant was properly discharged. The company relies on the evidence that grievant reported late for his scheduled turn . . . because he "slept in," as well as grievant's testimony that his failure to report timely was not related to any alcohol problem. Therefore, the company concludes that grievant had no Section 14-F rights in this case and that his discharge was otherwise for proper cause.

The arbitrator held for the company, ruling:

> The language of Section 14-F commits the company and the union to cooperate in encouraging employees afflicted with alcoholism and drug abuse to undergo rehabilitation programs; it does not preclude the company from otherwise imposing discipline for proper cause. Therefore, while a valid claim of alcoholism or drug abuse may operate as a mitigating circumstance in a given case, it is necessary that there be an adequate causal connection between the asserted affliction and the conduct which prompted the discipline.
>
> . . . [I]n the absence of a proven causal connection between grievant's admitted alcoholism and his failure to report timely for his scheduled turn . . . , it cannot be concluded that Section 14-F provides a proper basis for setting aside the discharge in this case.[9]

A similar result was reached in the case of a motor inspector helper who had been discharged for failing to report for work as scheduled. Before the discharge, in a period of more than two years, he had been suspended seven times for absenteeism or violation of the rules relating to "reporting off." During a lower level hearing, the union told the company that the grievant had an alcohol problem and that, in consequence, discharge was too severe a penalty.

In denying the grievance, the arbitrator wrote:

> Nothing else in the record prior to then hints at alcoholism as the reason for grievant's failure to be a more reliable employee. . . . Grievant himself did not offer any testimony on . . . efforts [at rehabilitation] except to say that he had quit drinking. The report of the company physician . . . indicated that on the basis of a medical examination, the doctor concluded that grievant was not an alcoholic. For these reasons, the board finds that Section 14-F . . . is not pertinent to a consideration of the case.
>
> Perhaps it should be noted here, however, that Section 14-F is neither a sword nor a shield in the imposition of discipline, but rather an expression of the parties' *mutual* desire to help individual employees seeking to overcome a grave and unfortunate problem. The duties assumed by the parties necessarily rest upon a frank recognition of the victim's alcoholism as early as possible so that a sustained effort at rehabilitation is possible.[10]

In both of these steel cases, there was some doubt about whether the grievant was a bona fide alcoholic. But even when alcoholism has been established, the board has held, a discharge may be sustained if the underlying condition is not directly related to the conduct for which the discipline was imposed. Thus, in a case in which the grievant was discharged for failure to "report off" properly, the arbitrator found that the grievant was "afflicted with alcohol" abuse but that

> [t]he infraction for which he was discharged was not caused by the consumption of alcohol or any indisposition caused by alcoholism. Thus, the inquiry is reduced to the question of whether grievant's general abuse of alcohol sufficiently mitigates against discharge under all circumstances of this case.
>
> Grievant has a very short tenure with the company. While absenteeism is consistent with the work record of an alcoholic, . . . it cannot be determined whether his prior infractions were caused by his abuse of alcohol . . . [and] no evidence was presented to show that the company should have suspected that grievant had any problem. . . . The grievance is denied.[11]

The Employee's Prior Record

A related issue is the extent to which an employee's efforts at rehabilitation preclude consideration of his prior record. A rollhand with a poor disciplinary record underwent treatment for alcoholism for about a month as a result of company–union efforts at the local level. He returned to work and was, in the opinion of the union, maintaining sobriety. Several months later, however, he was discharged as the result of an incident in which he failed to "report off" before his scheduled shift began. After dismissing the grievant's explanation of the failure—the employee claimed to have suffered a severe bronchial attack on the way to work—the arbitrator turned to the union's assertion that the grievant's "discipline record prior to his undergoing treatment for control of alcoholism should be disregarded in light of his successful efforts to rehabilitate himself." The arbitrator held:

> The union's position that his record prior to undergoing treatment should be *disregarded*, because of its relationship to his alcoholic problem and in light of the subsequent improvement in his record, cannot be endorsed by the board, although the board agrees that those factors pointed out by the union are entitled to *due consideration* for purposes of evaluating his overall record.[12]

After due consideration, the arbitrator concluded that the employer had proper cause for the discharge.

An employee's attempts to rehabilitate himself may be taken into account if he subsequently develops additional dependencies. In one case, the grievant, who was a janitor, had undergone a residential alcoholism treatment program, apparently successfully, and had then returned to work for a prolonged period, attracting no discipline other than a warning for a safety rule violation. However, he went on sick leave for a back disorder and during that period developed a drug dependency from prescribed painkillers. He also began drinking again. He started in a drug detoxification program but stopped prematurely because of a financial need to resume working. A few months later, he was discharged for reporting late for work without proper notification. The employer argued that it had already fulfilled its obligation under Section 14-F to give the grievant an opportunity for rehabilitation. Reviewing the record, the arbitrator concluded:

> There is no indication in the present evidence that, when [the grievant] returned to work . . . , the local parties focussed at all on the problems he had developed. . . . If the full facts had been known to the appropriate persons, presumably efforts would have been made under Section 14-F to further assist grievant's rehabilitation.
>
> . . . [T]he relevant circumstances in this case include grievant's relatively good record in the period after he underwent his initial rehabilitation almost two years prior to his discharge and the fact that the specific infraction which triggered his discharge

was both related to his alcohol and drug problem and not particularly egregious in nature.

> . . . The Board agrees with the union's contention that he should have been afforded an opportunity in which to participate in a coordinated alcohol and drug rehabilitation program. . . . Grievant is to be reinstated . . . and the period between his discharge and reinstatement is to be treated as a leave of absence.[13]

"Last Chance" Agreements

On occasion, an employer and a discharged employee may sign a "rehabilitation agreement" or "last chance agreement," under which the employer voluntarily reinstates the employee in return for a pledge to enter treatment as well as improve job performance. Usually, the employee agrees that should he violate the terms, either by failing to remain in treatment or by further misconduct at work, he will be terminated. Such an agreement was witnessed by company and union representatives in the case of Andy Y. (see "Andy Y.: A Case Study" in Chapter 1):

CONDITION OF EMPLOYMENT

I understand that my reinstatement to employment by the corporation is based upon and constrained by the following terms:

1. I accept admission to the Employee Assistance Program.
2. I recognize that my reinstatement is contingent upon the participation of my spouse and adult children in my recovery through the Employee Assistance Program.
3. I will comply with ALL of the program agreement requirements to their successful conclusion.
4. I recognize the adverse impact that working overtime may have on my recovery and waive my rights to assignment to overtime. For the same reason, I will accept supervision's decisions regarding requests for payment in lieu of vacation time off.
5. I understand that my previous job performance warrants close supervision for an extended period of time upon my return to work and will accept such supervision as a constructive part of my recovery.
6. I understand that upon return to the workplace I must meet all established standards of conduct and job performance and that I will be subject to the company's disciplinary procedures for any failure to meet the standards.
7. I understand that I will be subject to the terms of this condition of employment until I have completed at least

twelve months of work. Upon completion of twelve months of work the appropriate parties will review my job performance and recovery progress and determine if the terms of this condition of employment will be removed, modified, sustained, or added to.

I UNDERSTAND AND AGREE THAT MY REINSTATEMENT AND CONTINUED EMPLOYMENT ARE CONTINGENT UPON MY MEETING SATISFACTORILY ALL THE ABOVE TERMS OF THIS CONDITION OF EMPLOYMENT AND THAT MY FAILURE TO DO SO RELINQUISHES ALL DEFENSE ON MY PART AND SUBJECTS ME TO IMMEDIATE TERMINATION OF MY EMPLOYMENT WITH THE CORPORATION.

The same employee also entered into a program agreement:

I, Andy, fully understand and agree to the terms of my total participation in the corporation Employee Assistance Program. This program may include, but is not limited to:

1. Detoxification in the designated facility for a designated time according to my needs;
2. Returning to work immediately after detoxification and/or residential treatment (hospital or other) in accordance with the appropriate procedures;
3. Attending a minimum of four . . . meetings of Alcoholics Anonymous (AA). One weekly meeting will be the AA Sunday night meeting[;]
4. Keeping weekly counseling and consultation appointments with the counselor[;]
5. When requested, providing the medical director [with] the information necessary (including required releases of information) for him to assess my medical status [and] to consult with other medical resources such as my personal physician concerning my treatment and recovery;
6. Making sincere efforts to recover from my alcoholism with the understanding that failure to adhere to this agreement exhausts all help available to me through the program, and that I will continue to be subject to the company's disciplinary procedures, not for my alcoholism, but based on the effect the continuation of alcoholism may have on my job performance and work behavior[.]
7. Persons participating in the program are expected to meet existing job performance standards and established work rules. No preferential treatment is shown employees on program.
8. In the event I do not abide by the above, I realize there will be no additional opportunity to return to the program.

The employee's wife also agreed to the following family program agreement:

I, spouse of Andy, fully understand and agree to all terms of family participation in the Employee Assistance Program.

This program will include:

1. Compliance with all facets of family treatment offered during spouse's stay at treatment center;
2. Compliance with all facets of . . . after care sponsored by the treatment center;
3. Keeping weekly counseling and consultation appointments with the counselor;
4. Attending a minimum of 3 Al-Anon meetings weekly, one of which will be the Al-Anon Sunday night weekly meeting.

Validity of Agreements

The validity of last chance agreements is sometimes challenged in arbitration by grievants who have subsequently been discharged for violating them. The arguments in favor of upholding such a discharge have been cogently summarized by an arbitrator in the case of a grievant with a history of both alcoholism and drug abuse:

> [S]pecial agreements of the "last chance" gender . . . are enforceable. This is true for two reasons.
>
> First of all, last chance agreements are supported by consideration and may, therefore, be taken as a modification of the master collective bargaining agreement, in their application to special employees. The company gives valuable consideration . . . by giving up a contended right to discharge an employee at the time reinstatement is made. . . .
>
> Secondly, last chance agreements are supported as a matter of public policy. They serve a useful social function of salvaging . . . employees whose jobs would otherwise be lost. Many times, the impact of a "last chance" agreement will have sufficient shock value to rehabilitate an errant employee. If arbitrators did not enforce last chance agreements, employers would cease to enter them, and the beneficial social purpose which they serve would be lost to society generally and to members of the bargaining unit specifically.[14]

Related Issues

Under a last chance agreement, an employee may also waive his right to appeal through the grievance procedure in the event of another infraction involving drinking. Should there be, then, presumption of nonarbitrability in any future alcohol-related discharge proceedings? Unions often argue that side agreements which waive appeal rights should be overturned or modified on the ground that they were made "under duress" by employees fearful of losing their jobs. This argument overlooks the "consideration" that was given by the employer when rescinding the previous discharge; nevertheless, as a practical matter, the question of whether the last chance agreement was properly invoked under the facts and circumstances alleged by the employer typically would remain arbitrable.

Another issue presented by the last chance agreement is whether it establishes a past practice whose benefits can be claimed by other alcoholic employees threatened with immediate discharge. The agreements often assert that they set no precedent for future alcohol-related discipline cases. Yet, after agreements have been signed with a number of employees, an arbitrator may be called upon to decide whether disclaiming the intention to set a precedent can erase the plain fact that the employer has customarily offered alcoholic employees a last chance agreement.

Conclusion

This volume has dealt with a wide spectrum of issues relating to alcohol and drugs. Summarizing a discussion that covered so many topics would be difficult, but a few general observations seem in order.

There is no lack of willingness on the part of arbitrators to try to accommodate the notion of "just cause" to the reality of alcoholism. The question that still bedevils the arbitral process, though, is how to avoid either wrenching arbitrators out of the deliberately circumscribed role that they have traditionally played—with all the dangers and uncertainties that entails—or subjecting alcoholic employees to a process unlikely to deal adequately with their condition. It is a question which may ultimately be answered by the accumulation of experience, but until then parties should take account of these limitations before they bring to arbitration a case involving a grievant who is an alcoholic.

For now, there seems to be an emerging consensus among arbitrators, advocates and treatment specialists that the normal progression of corrective discipline should not be suspended for the alcoholic employee. On the contrary, the alcoholic should be held accountable for his conduct, but, to be truly "corrective," disciplinary penalties should be coupled with opportunities to recover. In reviewing the imposition of discipline, the arbitrator might take into consideration such factors as how much reason there was for the employer to know that the employee was an alcoholic, how much assistance was offered the employee and how well the employee took advantage of the assistance that was offered. All of these, no doubt, are to be measured in degrees, but assigning relative weight to a variety of decisional factors is a familiar task for arbitrators.

Obviously, such decisions are made easier when an employee's alcoholism is recognized before his conduct has led to a discharge. There is no dispute that an alcoholic is ultimately dischargeable for misconduct or poor performance. As even the "Big Book," the bible of Alcoholics Anonymous, says to employers: "If he wants to stop [drinking], he should be afforded a real chance. If he cannot or does not want to stop, he should be discharged."[1] The question is, what is a "real chance"?

Where an arbitrator believes that reinstatement is warranted, it would be well to bear in mind the lesson illustrated by the case of Andy Y.—that reinstatement, unaccompanied by constructive measures to deal with the employee's alcoholism, is not a realistic outcome. Reinstatement alone tends merely to delay the employee's inevitable termination, and it may cause harm by enabling self-destructive drinking to continue. The challenge is to devise reinstatement arrangements which are not unduly onerous but which ensure that the "second chance" is meaningful.

Employee Assistance Programs have a large part to play in affording an alcoholic an opportunity for recovery. Their role should be recognized in the arbitration process, and "due process" arguments which might thwart their proper functioning should be scrutinized carefully. Ideally, no discharge case should arrive at the arbitration stage before there has been an effort to have the Employee Assistance Program deal with the problems which underlie the behavior that led to the discipline.

If a discharge occurs before the employee's alcoholism is recognized, a fruitful alternative to arbitration might be for union and management to agree to stay the termination while the employee makes an intensive attempt at recovery, such as in a residential treatment facility covered by the health benefit plan. At the very least, unions should try to persuade alcoholic employees to seek treatment during the often substantial interval between the discharge and the arbitration.[2]

The workplace suffers not only from employee alcoholism but, as we have seen, from employee abuse of alcohol on the job, either by employees' coming to work intoxicated or by their drinking while working. However, the resulting disciplinary measures often lead to unnecessary disputes because employer rules are neither comprehensive nor specific nor properly disseminated to the workforce in advance. Glaring flaws include the failure to specify what is meant by such phrases as "under the influence" and the omission of objective standards, particularly the maximum permissible blood alcohol concentration.

The same strictures apply *a fortiori* when employees are accused of being under the influence of drugs. Owing to the enormous variety of drugs that are commonly abused, not only the level of intoxication but the very identity of the drug is often in dispute.

Some of this conflict might be avoided if the rules against substance abuse, wherever compatible with the needs of individual industries, were to be drawn in terms of impairment. The issue in arbitration then would become whether the employee was working or reporting for work while "impaired," that is, unable to perform his duties safely and effectively. The impairment standard could be coupled with progressive discipline culminating in discharge after warnings and suspensions for a series of similar infractions.

The impairment standard would offer a number of advantages in both alcohol and drug cases. The nature of the substance used and the level of the dosage would no longer be critical issues; establishing impairment does not necessarily require interpretation of arcane laboratory procedures, and the eyewitness evidence of those working with the grievant normally would suffice. Moreover, by adopting a scale of discipline, rather than imposing summary discharge even for a first offense, the incentive for "cover-ups"—by fellow employees or even supervisors—would probably diminish.

The stakes in arbitration—and the tension at the hearing—also would be reduced considerably. It is clear that in reviewing a discharge for a single disciplinary infraction, arbitrators are extremely sensitive to imperfections in the case against the employee, especially one with long service. A graduated scale of disciplinary measures for repeated instances of impairment would tend to obviate such painful decisions, yet would still serve to screen out those employees who persistently abuse alcohol and drugs. The scale would also make it easier to identify employees whose jobs could be saved if they were offered treatment before their poor performance led to discharge.

In the case of drugs, the impairment standard would shift the focus profitably from such questions as whether an employee is an "addict." The label of "addict" tends to carry many unexamined notions and some sheer myths. Drug abuse is widespread, but its intensity ranges from the recreational to the pathological, and the properties of drugs are enormously varied. If inferences are to be drawn about an employee's drug use, the pattern of involvement and the nature of the drug should be clearly documented.

It should also be remembered that "drugs" are not synonymous with "illegal drugs." The majority of abused substances are medicines that are legally prescribed, yet the legal status of the drug is often the critical factor in determining disciplinary penalties. The workplace should, of course, be free of criminal activities, such as the distribution of illegal drugs. But the primary concern of industry is for safety and productivity, and the disciplinary structure should reflect the fact that these are jeopardized as much by legal as by illegal substances.

Finally, a review of the history of alcohol and drug arbitration argues powerfully for joint approaches to the problem through the collective bargaining agreement. Many disputes can be precluded by agreeing in advance on reasonable rules against substance abuse and a fair system for enforcing them. Management and labor also have good reason to offer rehabilitative options to those identified as alcoholics and drug abusers, intervening before severe disciplinary sanctions need to be invoked. Given the mutual stake of both management and labor in creating a wholesome work environment, there is a strong common interest in reducing the level of industrial conflict over substance abuse and making a mutual effort to eliminate it.

Appendix A

Abused Drugs and Their Symptoms*

Narcotic Analgesics

Narcotic analgesics relieve pain, induce sedation or sleep and elevate mood, particularly when it is depressed. They also suppress cough and are constipating. A high degree of tolerance and severe physical and psychological dependence usually develop with prolonged or repeated use. The withdrawal syndrome is severe and uncomfortable. Overdosage causes death by respiratory depression. Most of the symptoms can be ascribed to abnormal functions of the autonomic nervous system.

These drugs have been taken by mouth, sniffed, injected subcutaneously or intravenously and smoked (opium).

Nalorphine (Nalline) and levallorphan (Lortan) are synthetic narcotic antagonists which themselves can cause drug dependence.

Examples of widely abused narcotic analgesics are: opium, morphine, heroin, laudanum, paregoric, codeine, meperidine (Demerol) and methadone (Dolophine).

Diagnosis

Behavioral

- Euphoria
- Drowsiness
- Nodding
- Loss of appetite and sexual drive
- Altered personality and activity
- Lack of attentiveness

**Source: Desk Reference on Drug Misuse and Abuse,* State of New York Division of Substance Abuse Services and New York State Medical Society, 1981.

Physical

- Pinpoint pupils (less in seasoned addicts or with some opioids)
- Itchy nose and skin
- Needle tracks of extremities, groin and abdomen which may resemble pock marks in addicts using subcutaneous route
- Nausea and vomiting
- Slow pulse and respiration
- Respiratory failure
- Constipation

Laboratory

If intake is within 8–10 hours, these drugs can be readily detected in blood (10cc, unclotted) and urine (2 oz.); with better techniques, up to 24 hours and longer.

Propoxyphene HCL (Darvon)

May be taken orally or intravenously "mainline".

Diagnosis

Behavioral and physical signs and symptoms resemble heroin overdose with prominent signs of gastric irritation. Grand mal seizures indistinguishable from epilepsy may occur as part of the abuse symptom or from abstinence.

Pentazocine, HCL or Lactate (Talwin)

More commonly abused when other narcotic sources dry up. Most often, the tablets are dissolved (IV or IM) with tripelennamine (Pyribenzamine) or other antihistamines on a 3:1 ratio. Narcotic abusers find this formula gives a "high" (euphoria) similar to 3 bags of heroin + 1 cap of cocaine. Unfortunately, Pyribenzamine tablets both contain talc (as do many tablets), and this foreign substance induces a necrotizing angitis or soft tissue destruction from repeated administration.

Diagnosis

Same as for other narcotics.

Physical Effects

Same as other narcotics and gangrenous destruction of tissue where injected.

Central Nervous System Stimulants

These drugs produce excitatory effects in the central nervous system, characterized by increased wakefulness, alertness, feelings of increased initiative and ability, and depression of appetite. Excessive dosage, particularly when administered intravenously ("speed"), produces a delirious or psychotic state. The period of excitement or stimulation is followed by an after-depression. This tends to set off self-perpetuating use of these drugs in binges. Tolerance develops rapidly, sometimes accompanied by psychological dependence. The occurrence of physical dependence with a clearcut abstinence syndrome is highly questionable.

Signs and symptoms of peripheral sympathetic nervous stimulation complicate the picture of the intoxication.

The drugs are usually ingested, but may also be sniffed (cocaine), injected intravenously (amphetamine-speed), and smoked or "skin-popped" (subcutaneous injection).

Amphetamines and Amphetamine-Like Drugs

- Methedrine, Crystal (methamphetamine)
- Dexamyl (dextroamphetamine and amobarbital)
- Eskatrol (dextroamphetamine and prochlorperazine)
- Preludin (phenmetrazine hydrochloride)
- Biphetamine-20 (amphetamine 10 mg.: dextroamphetamine 10 mg.)
- Tenuate, Tepanil (diethylpropion hydrochloride)
- Ionamin (phenteramine resin)
- Sanorex (mazindol)
- Pondimin (fenfluramine hydrochloride)
- Desoxyn (methamphetamine)
- Fastin (phenteramine HCL)
- Ritalin (methylphenidate)
- Cocaine

Diagnosis

Behavioral

- Wakeful
- Alert
- Talkative
- Abnormal cheerfulness
- Increased initiative
- Increased motor activity
- Irritability, restlessness
- Aggressiveness, agitation, pruritus
- May have hallucinations and paranoid tendencies, especially with substantial sleep deprivation
- Severe depression when the effects wear off; then suicidal tendencies may emerge

Physical

- Tremor
- Dry mouth
- Bad breath
- Tachycardia, hypertension (may be absent in chronic user)
- Malnutrition (in chronic users)
- Sweating
- Needle marks ("speed freak")
- Dilated pupils
- Fever
- Hyperreflexia
- Arrhythmias (usually pre-ventricular contractions)
- Palpitations
- Convulsions
- Coma in fatal poisoning
- Circulatory collapse

Laboratory

Possible to identify these drugs in blood or urine samples.

Cocaine

Diagnosis

Behavioral

- Garrulousness
- Shudders

- Brief euphoria
- Feeling of mental & physical superiority
- May have depression or hallucinations
- Aggressiveness may signal oncoming violence
- Paranoid psychosis

Physical

- Perforated nasal septum in sniffer
- Muscle twitching
- Hyperactive reflexes
- Rapid pulse
- Irregular respirations
- Numbness of hands and feet
- Failure of sight and hearing
- Cyanosis
- Convulsions
- Coma
- Repiratory paralysis

Laboratory

Blood and urine levels may be of assistance.

Central Nervous System Depressants

These drugs produce general, progressive depression of the central nervous system, characterized by sedation and sleep, sometimes preceded by a period of apparent excitement and disinhibition. In overdose, they cause coma and death by respiratory failure. The effects of all drugs in this class are mutually addictive, including those of alcohol.

Physical and psychological dependence may develop on prolonged or repeated use; the withdrawal syndrome is characteristically different from and more serious than that produced by narcotic analgesics. There is cross-tolerance and cross-dependence among all drugs in this class.

These drugs are usually taken by mouth, but occasionally are injected or inhaled.

Barbiturates

Drugs Abused More Commonly

- Amobarbital (Amytal)
- Combined Amobarbital and Secobarbital (Tuinal)

- Pentobarbital (Nembutal)
- Secobarbital (Seconal)
- Butalbital (Fiorinal)

Drugs Abused Less Commonly

- Barbital (Veronal)
- Butabarbital (Butisol)
- Hexobarbital (Evipal)
- Phenobarbital (Luminal)
- Thiopental (Pentothal)

Diagnosis—Overdose

Behavioral

- Drowsiness
- Drunken behavior
- Confusion
- Irritability
- Inattentiveness

Physical

- Weak pulse, rapid or slow
- Hypotension
- Reduction of reflexes
- Ataxia
- Slurred speech
- Lowered temperature

Diagnosis—Withdrawal

Behavioral (12–24 hours after last dose)

- Anorexia
- Anxiety
- Abdominal cramps
- Headaches
- Hyperreflexia
- Insomnia
- Nausea and vomiting

Physical

- Diaphoresis
- Hypotension

- Grand mal seizures (2–7 days after last dose)
- Delirium (4–6 days after last dose)

Methaqualone

- Quaalude
- Maquin
- Parest
- Sopor
- Mandrake

Diagnosis

See Barbiturates.

Glutethimide (Doriden)

The effects of this drug closely resemble those of the barbiturates. It may, however, cause severe and unexpected hypotension.

Diagnosis

See Barbiturates.
Hypotension may be prominent.

Laboratory

Drug can be identified in 10 cc unclotted blood or 2 oz. urine.

Chloral Hydrate

Diagnosis

Signs and symptoms resemble those of acute barbiturate intoxication. They may be accompanied by marked gastric irritation and vomiting.

Other Sedatives and Anti-Anxiety Agents

Minor Tranquilizers

Meprobamate (Miltown or Equanil), methyprylon (Noludar), ethinamate (Valmid), ethchlorvynol (Placidyl). If greater than 4 times recommended daily dose abused for longer than 30 days, generally wise to hospitalize for gradual detoxification.

Diagnosis

The signs and symptoms closely resemble those of acute barbiturate intoxication, but severe hypotension may develop at any time during the clinical course, sometimes without correlation to the severity of the behavioral symptoms.

Laboratory

Blood levels may be determined but their significance is uncertain.

Anti-Anxiety Agents

Benzodiazepines (Librium, Valium, Tranxene, Azene)

Anti-anxiety drugs are indicated when anxiety causes the patient genuine suffering and interferes with general functioning of job performance or ability to relate to people. Since these drugs are subject to abuse; and their misuse may hinder the development of personal coping strategies or the effective mobilization of social support systems within the family or community, one may consider using constraint in the prescribing of these agents. In addition, anti-anxiety drugs may well obscure the basic source of the presenting anxiety.

Diagnosis

Physical

- Severely ill patients with signs of respiratory failure
- Possible convulsions on rapid withdrawal
- Cyanosis
- Constriction of pupils (unless anoxic)
- Reduction of urinary output

Laboratory

Blood levels may be of value in prognosis: 10 cc of unclotted blood required; 2 oz. of urine for thin-layer chromatography.

Hallucinogens

These drugs produce a toxic delirium characterized by visual illusions and hallucinations, and sometimes accompanied by disturbances in proprioception, bizarre paresthesias and synesthesias, perceptual distortions, etc. Auditory hallucinations are less common. There may also be difficulties in concentration. Changes in affect may range from hilarity to depression or panic states. The central nervous system effects may be complicated by peripheral autonomic effects. The duration and intensity of these effects vary a great deal from drug to drug and individual to individual. Tolerance occurs with some drugs; psychological dependence may occur occasionally, but there are no clear-cut signs of physical dependence.

LSD (D-lysergic acid diethylamide)

Usually taken orally on sugar cube, blotter paper, cookie, etc. Occasionally injected intravenously. Often used in group setting.

Diagnosis

Behavioral

- Duration, 8-12 hours, with possible recurrence of "trip" even after prolonged periods of abstinence
- "Trip" is characterized by hallucinations, largely visual
- Distortion of sensory perception
- Exaggerated sense of comprehension: may "see" smells, "hear" colors
- False sense of achievement, ability and strength
- Loss of sense of reality
- Suggestibility
- Depersonalization, alteration of body image
- Tends to intensify existing psychosis
- May trigger suicidal tendencies
- For some, panic and violence may be present; others experience a lessened anxiety and feelings of a deep and transcendental experience

Physical

- Pupils dilated
- Incoordination
- Moderate tachycardia
- Numbness, tingling, nausea may occur
- Mild hypertension
- Eyes may become inflamed

Other Hallucinogens

The other hallucinogens listed below differ from LSD in potency and duration of action but not in regard to the quality of their effects on the central nervous system. The diagnosis and treatment of intoxications are, therefore, virtually identical to LSD.

- Mushrooms (psilocybin): Duration, 5–8 hours; swallowed.
- Peyote (mescaline, synthetic compound found in peyote): Duration: 8–12 hours; swallowed or occasionally injected.
- DET (diethyltriptamine): Duration, 2–3 hours; smoked or injected.
- DMT (dimethyltriptamine): Duration, 1–3 hours; smoked or injected.
- DOM or "STP" (dimethyoxy methylamphetamine): Synthetic effects similar to mescaline and amphetamine. Duration: 2–4 days, swallowed.
- Morning glory seeds (Rivea Corimbosa): Only 1/10th as strong as LSD. Duration: variable; seeds chewed or made into a tea.
- MDA (methylene dioxyamphetamine), The "love drug": In minute doses resembles LSD, in larger doses highly toxic. Taken by mouth in capsules. Little valid information available.

Diagnosis

Same as for LSD.

PCP (phencyclidine)

Formerly used as an animal tranquilizer (Sernyl); "street" names are Peace Pill, hog, rhino, angel dust.

Diagnosis

Behavioral

- Duration: 8–12 hours or longer
- May have short-lasting hallucinations as with other hallucinogens or may have appearance of thought disorder (schizophrenia)

- Autistic, ambivalent affect—labile and inappropriate; associations—loose
- May become catatonic or violently paranoid, commonly with religious overtones to their delusions
- Violent, psychotic behavior may last several days or weeks after one "hit" of this drug
- Status epilepticus, coma and death may occur

Physical

Same as other hallucinogens, plus vertical and horizontal nystagmus.

Laboratory

May detect drug by urine testing as long as 5 days after ingestion.

Volatile Hydrocarbons and Petroleum Derivatives

These substances include glue, gasoline, benzene, carbon tetrachloride, nail polish remover, aerosols, lighter fluid, paint, lacquer and varnish thinner. (NOTE: patient may present as unconscious, or DOA, with plastic bag over head, indicating use of inhalants.)

Diagnosis

Behavioral

- Hazy euphoria
- Slurred speech
- Impaired perception, coordination and judgement
- Initial excitation may be followed by depression and stupor
- Hallucinations in 50% of cases
- Occasional psychotic outburst
- Every day use for 6 months duration or longer may cause irreversible brain damage; diagnosed by psychological testing for organicity and/or C.A.T. Scan

Physical

- Odor
- Rapid pulse
- Damage of brain, liver, kidneys, bone marrow and myocardium

- Possible ventricular tachycardia or fibrillation
- Freon propellant in aerosols may cause freezing in nasopharynx
- Anoxia by replacing pulmonary air

Laboratory

Relevant to determine tissue damage (SGOT)

Belladonna Alkaloids

Belladonna, hyoscyamine, stramonium, atropine, homatropine, and particularly scopolamine, all produce central nervous system depression which is often preceded by a period of apparent stimulation and delirium. The effects of large doses are very long lasting.

Remember that substances such as morning glory seeds and many over-the-counter preparations contain belladonna alkaloids.

Diagnosis

Behavioral

- Classical: "Hot as a hare, red as a beet, mad as a hatter"
- Weakness
- Giddiness
- Thirst
- Blurred vision
- Great excitement and confusion
- Delirium
- Stupor
- Coma

Physical

- Dry mouth and throat
- Dilated pupils
- Twitching
- Difficult swallowing
- Light sensitivity
- Elevation of temperature and blood pressure
- Pulse: first slow, then rapid and weak
- Respiratory depression
- Cyanosis
- Urinary retention

Alcohol Abuse

Alcohol Intoxication

Symptoms

- Varying degrees of exhilaration and excitement
- Irregular behavior
- Loss of restraint
- Slurred speech
- Incoordination of movement and gait
- Drowsiness
- May progress to stupor and coma

Acute Phase

On rare occasions acute intoxication is characterized by an outburst of combative, irrational, and destructive behavior which terminates when the patient falls into deep stupor for which they have no memory. This state has been referred to as "pathological intoxication." Allegedly, this reaction may follow the ingestion of relatively small amounts of alcohol. "Blackouts" in the language of ETOHers refer to transient episodes of amnesia which accompany heavy intoxi cation. After the patient becomes sober, he cannot recall events that had occurred over a period of several hours even though the state of consciousness was not severely altered during this period.

Alcohol Withdrawal

May occur in any patient regardless of pattern of alcohol consumption when alcohol consumption is reduced or stopped abruptly.

Routine Withdrawal

May occur a few hours to 10 days after the last drink.

Behavioral

- Agitation
- Anorexia
- Impaired concentration
- Impaired memory

- Insomnia
- Irritability
- Perceptual disorders
- Nightmares
- Restlessness

Physical

(Symptoms are not time specific and may occur in any progression)

- Hypertension
- Nausea and vomiting
- Conjunctival injection
- Sweating
- Tachycardia
- Tremors

Laboratory

- Serum blood alcohol
- Breathalyzer

Appendix B

Glossary of "Street Names" for Drugs*

Amphetamines—Beans, Bennies, Black Beauties, Blackbirds, Black Mollies, Bumblebees, Cartwheels, Chalk, Chicken Powder, Copilots, Crank, Crossroads, Crystal, Dexies, Double Cross, Eye Openers, Hearts, Jelly Beans, Lightning, Meth, Minibennies, Nuggets, Oranges, Pep Pills, Speed, Roses, Thrusters, Truck Drivers, Turnabouts, Uppers, Ups, Wake-ups

Barbiturates—Barbs, Block Busters, Bluebirds, Blue Devils, Blues, Christmas Trees, Downers, Green Dragons, Marshmallow Reds, Mexican Reds, Nebbies, Nimbies, Peanuts, Pink Ladies, Pinks, Rainbows, Red and Blues, Redbirds, Red Devils, Reds, Sleeping Pills, Stumblers, Yellow Jackets, Yellows

Cocaine—Bernice, Bernies, Big C, Blow, C, Coke, Dream, Flake, Girl, Gold Dust, Heaven Dust, Nose Candy, Paradise, Rock, Snow, White

Glutethimide—C.D., Cibas

Hashish—Black Russian, Hash, Kif, Quarter Moon, Soles

Heroin—Big H, Boy, Brown, Brown Sugar, Caballo, Chinese Red, Chiva, Crap, Doojee, H, Harry, Horse, Junk, Mexican Mud, Powder, Scag, Smack, Stuff, Thing

LSD—Acid, Beast, Big D, Blue Cheer, Blue Heaven, Blue Mist, Brown Dots, California Sunshine, Chocolate Chips, Coffee,

*Source: *Drugs of Abuse,* U.S. Department of Justice, Drug Enforcement Administration.

Contact Lens, Cupcakes, Haze, Mellow Yellows, Microdots, Orange Mushrooms, Orange Wedges, Owsley, Paper Acid, Royal Blue, Strawberry Fields, Sugar, Sunshine, The Hawk, Wedges, White Lightning, Window Pane, Yellows

Marihuana—Acapulco Gold, Broccoli, Bush, Dry High, Gage, Ganga, Grass, Griffo, Hay, Hemp, Herb, J, Jay, Jane, Mary Jane, Mota, Mutah, Panama Red, Pod, Pot, Reefer, Sativa, Smoke, Stick, Tea, Weed

MDA—Love Drug

Mescaline—Beans, Buttons, Cactus, Mesc, Mescal, Mescal Buttons, Moon

Methamphetamines—Crystal, Meth, Speed

Methaqualone—Quas, Quads, Soapers, Sopes

Morphine—Cube, First Line, Hocus, Miss Emma, Morf, Morpho, Morphy, Mud

Phencyclidine—Angel Dust, DOA (Dead On Arrival), Hog, Killer Weed (when combined with marihuana or other plant material), PCP, Peace Pill

Psilocybin/Psilocyn—Magic Mushroom, Mushroom

Appendix C

Summary of the Controlled Substances Act*

Procedures for Controlling Substances

The purpose of the Federal Controlled Substances Act (CSA) is to minimize the quantity of drugs of abuse which are available to persons who are prone to abuse drugs. Procedures for controlling a substance under the CSA are set forth in Section 201 of the Act. Proceedings may be initiated by the Department of Health, Education, and Welfare (HEW), by DEA, or by petition from any interested person. This may be manufacturer, a medical society or association, a pharmacy association, a public interest group, a state or local government agency, or an individual citizen. When a petition is received by DEA, the agency begins its own investigation of the drug.

The Controlled Substances Act sets forth the findings which must be made to put a substance in any of the five schedules. These are as follows (Section 202(b)):

Schedule I

(A) The drug or other substance has a high potential for abuse.

(B) The drug or other substance has no currently accepted medical use in treatment in the United States.

(C) There is a lack of accepted safety for use of the drug or other substance under medical supervision.

---

*Source: *Drugs of Abuse*, U.S. Department of Justice, Drug Enforcement Administration.

Schedule II

(A) The drug or other substance has a high potential for abuse.
(B) The drug or other substance has a currently accepted medical use in treatment in the United States or a currently accepted medical use with severe restrictions.
(C) Abuse of the drug or other substances may lead to severe psychological or physical dependence.

Schedule III

(A) The drug or other substance has a potential for abuse less than the drugs or other substances in Schedules I and II.
(B) The drug or other substance has a currently accepted medical use in treatment in the United States.
(C) Abuse of the drug or other substance may lead to moderate or low physical dependence or high psychological dependence.

Schedule IV

(A) The drug or other substance has a low potential for abuse relative to the drugs or other substances in Schedule III.
(B) The drug or other substance has a currently accepted medical use in treatment in the United States.
(C) Abuse of the drug or other substance may lead to limited physical dependence or psychological dependence relative to the drugs or other substances in Schedule III.

Schedule V

(A) The drug or other substance has a low potential for abuse relative to the drugs or other substances in Schedule IV.
(B) The drug or other substance has a currently accepted medical use in treatment in the United States.
(C) Abuse of the drug or other substance may lead to limited physical dependence or psychological dependence relative to the drugs or other substances in Schedule IV.

In making these findings, DEA and HEW are directed to consider eight specific factors (Section 201(c)):

(1) Its actual or relative potential for abuse;
(2) Scientific evidence of its pharmacological effect, if known;

(3) The state of current scientific knowledge regarding the drug or other substance;

(4) Its history and current pattern of abuse;

(5) The scope, duration, and significance of abuse;

(6) What, if any, risk there is to the public health;

(7) Its psychic or physiological dependence liability;

(8) Whether the substance is an immediate precursor of a substance already controlled under this title.

A key criterion for controlling a substance, and the one which will be used most often, is the substance's potential for abuse. If the Attorney General through his designee the Administrator determines that the data gathered and the evaluations and recommendations of the Secretary of HEW constitute substantial evidence of potential for abuse, he may initiate control proceedings under this section. Final control by the Attorney General will also be based on the Administrator's findings as to the substance's potential for abuse.

		Criminal Penalties for Trafficking (First Offense)	
Schedule	**Examples**	**Narcotic**	**Non-narcotic**
I	Heroin Marijuana Mescaline LSD	15 years/ $25,000	5 years/ $15,000
II	Opium Cocaine (classified as a narcotic) Methamphetamine	15 years/ $25,000	5 years/ $15,000
III	Codeine Other amphetamines Many barbiturates	5 years/ $15,000	5 years/ $15,000
IV	Phenobarbital Choral hydrate Meprobamate (Miltown)	3 years/ $10,000	3 years/ $10,000
V	Cough syrups containing codeine	1 year/ $5,000	1 year/ $5,000

Appendix D

Model Contract Language on Alcoholism and Drug Abuse Proposed by AFL-CIO*

I. Suggested Joint Policy Statement

The [union] and [company] jointly recognize alcoholism and drug abuse as illnesses which are treatable. It is also recognized that it is for the best interests of the employee, the [union] and the [company] that these illnesses be treated and controlled under the existing collective bargaining contractual relationship.

Our concern is limited to alcoholism and drug problems which cause poor attendance and unsatisfactory performance on the job. Our sole objective is to help not harm. This program is designed for rehabilitation and not elimination of the employee.

Any employee who participates in this program will be entitled to all of the rights and benefits provided to other employees who are sick, in addition to specific services and assistance which this program may provide.

It shall be the responsibility of all employees in a supervisory position to follow the joint union-management alcoholism and drugs problem policy and procedures. It shall also be their responsibility to assure any employee with an alcohol or drug problem that a request for diagnosis or treatment will not jeopardize his job rights or job security and that confidential handling of the diagnosis and treatment of these problems is an absolute fact—not just an assertion.

To coordinate a program and to implement this policy the [union] and the [company] agree to establish a joint committee on alcoholism and drug abuse at [location of facility]. If the program is company-wide, there should be a company-wide joint committee with local

---

**Source:* C. Schramm, *Development of Comprehensive Language on Alcoholism in Collective Bargaining Agreements*, 38 Journal of Studies on Alcohol 1405–27 (July 1977).

committees at each plant or other company facility. The company-wide committee would not be involved in any of the activities of the program requiring direct involvement in cases. However, the company-wide committee should:

1. Be composed of equal representation from management and the union. Preferably six or eight total committee membership.
2. Review the effectiveness of the program periodically. See that the reasonable uniformity is maintained.
3. Assist local committees with their problems when requested.
4. Check and report on suitability of medical and hospital facilities in each community and for each company facility.
5. Approve uniform training program for company supervisors and union stewards and union counselors.
6. Continue to seek means to improve over-all program, utilizing education, new developments and techniques, and assistance from agencies.
7. Engage in other activities (which the union and company approve) that will be beneficial to this program.

II. Local Joint Plant Committee on Alcoholism and Drug Abuse

The committee should be composed of four or six members. The union and the company shall have equal representation. One member shall serve as Committee Chairman. This office shall be rotated on a scheduled basis between the union and the company. Sufficient time shall be allowed the committee to develop a local plant program. (If there is a company-wide program the local program must be submitted to the company-wide committee for final clearance.)

This committee shall consider cases that are referred and review cases that are in process (subject to limitations pointed out in the section on procedures for case handling).

In addition this committee shall be responsible for developing and promoting educational information on the program, working with other agencies within the community who can assist in making programs more effective, developing procedures for referral to and use of community services for treatment, and making recommendations for program improvement.

III. Procedures for Case Handling

1. The earlier a drinking or drug abuse problem can be identified, the more favorable are the chances for a satisfactory solution.

2. The local plant committee will always be available to consider an alcohol or drug abuse case. The employee involved may directly make his own referral. Referrals may also be made by the supervisor or by the union representative.
3. When a supervisor, through daily job contact, observes an employee is experiencing difficulties in maintaining his performance, he will discuss the apparent difficulties with the employee. If the employee is unable to correct his job performance difficulties through his own efforts, the supervisor will notify the appropriate union representative and then arrange to offer the employee confidential assistance and services that are available as outlined in the following procedures.
4. The focus of corrective interviews is restricted to the issue of job performance and opinions or judgments on alcoholism or other drug use are prohibited. It must be re-emphasized that all referrals must be made on objective and factual bases rather than on any unsupported assumptions or judgments of the supervisor.
5. The employee(s) shall be afforded the right to have appropriate union representative(s) present at each such interview. In all instances the union representative(s) shall be notified that such an interview is scheduled.
6. If, following this discussion, it is felt by the supervisor, the employee, or his representative that the matter should be brought directly before the joint review committee, the committee chairman shall arrange a meeting as expeditiously as possible.

   At the meeting with the committee and the employee these steps should be taken:

   a. Give the employee a clear, positive statement pointing out all the evidence which indicates that a job performance problem is involved.
   b. Explain the function of the joint program and the benefits available in detail.
   c. Emphasize that help for the existing problem is covered under the program and handled on a confidential basis.
   d. Remind the employee that unless his problem is identified and corrected, he is subject to existing penalties for unsatisfactory job performance and attendance.
7. If the matter cannot be satisfactorily resolved by the joint review committee, disposition of the matter will proceed under the existing collective bargaining contractual relations between the union and the company.

IV. Treatment

It is recognized that supervisors, union representatives, and committee members are not professional diagnosticians in the field of alcoholism and drug abuse. Neither are they medical experts. However, the committee will select and approve the qualified physicians, therapists or personnel of other treatment resources and facilities whose recommendations for needed treatment and rehabilitation services will be followed.

V. Miscellaneous

It shall be the policy of the company to inform any employee subject to discharge or discipline, of his rights to a review before this committee to determine if the source of his problem falls within the corrective and treatment procedures offered by the program.

Appendix E

Table of Arbitration Cases on Alcohol and Drugs

The following table is a guide to locating cases published in the *Labor Arbitration Reports* that deal with discipline in cases involving alcohol or drugs. The table is organized according to the type of issue presented; since a case may involve more than one issue, some cases appear in more than one table. In general, the awards are classified as follows:

- Upheld: Employer's disciplinary action was fully sustained.
- Overruled: Grievance was fully sustained.
- Modified: Disciplinary penalty reduced or grievant reinstated with at least some loss of back pay.

A breakdown of the issues covered is given first to provide an overview.

A. Alcohol

A. Alcohol

1. Alcoholism

Upheld

21 LA 367 21 LA 452 41 LA 333 42 LA 1251 44 LA 308 45 LA 769
45 LA 932 47 LA 1029 48 LA 1187 49 LA 117 52 LA 195 54 LA 1091
56 LA 738 60 LA 1236 60 LA 1335 63 LA 274 63 LA 355 63 LA 618
67 LA 1145 67 LA 1296 70 LA 756 71 LA 737 72 LA 355 73 LA 1133
73 LA 228 74 LA 316 74 LA 641 75 LA 968 77 LA 448 77 LA 854
77 LA 1064 78 LA 302 79 LA 182

Overruled

24 LA 173 42 LA 408 56 LA 527 56 LA 789

Modified

39 LA 417 40 LA 935 44 LA 1043 52 LA 653 59 LA 334 65 LA 803
66 LA 965 67 LA 847 69 LA 811 71 LA 158 71 LA 445 72 LA 809
73 LA 1185 73 LA 1193 73 LA 1236 77 LA 775 79 LA 529 80 LA 193

2. Employee Assistance Program

Upheld

42 LA 1251 52 LA 195 63 LA 274 67 LA 1145 72 LA 355 73 LA 228
75 LA 896 75 LA 968 77 LA 854 77 LA 1064 78 LA 302 79 LA 182

Overruled

56 LA 789

Modified

66 LA 965 69 LA 811 72 LA 809 73 LA 1185 73 LA 1193 77 LA 775
79 LA 529

3. Post-Discharge Behavior

Upheld

42 LA 1251 45 LA 932 66 LA 1037 70 LA 756 71 LA 737 72 LA 355
74 LA 316 74 LA 641 77 LA 448 77 LA 1064 78 LA 302 79 LA 182

Overruled

42 LA 408 56 LA 527

Modified

40 LA 935 44 LA 1043 52 LA 653 71 LA 158 71 LA 445

4. "Last Chance" Agreements

Upheld

47 LA 1029 63 LA 274 63 LA 618 67 LA 1296 78 LA 302 79 LA 182

Modified

71 LA 158

5. Intoxication

Upheld

07 LA 292 19 LA 57 19 LA 733 21 LA 452 24 LA 810 30 LA 847
41 LA 1091 47 LA 1029 48 LA 1187 49 LA 564 52 LA 1279

Overruled

02 LA 305 02 LA 384 11 LA 195 18 LA 336 27 LA 128 31 LA 832
41 LA 1083 41 LA 888 60 LA 1030 63 LA 1102

Modified

03 LA 880 07 LA 704 08 LA 97 38 LA 602 40 LA 717 78 LA 1060

6. Searches

Upheld

50 LA 173 68 LA 702

Alcohol—Searches, contd.

Overruled

48 LA 567

Modified

58 LA 279

7. Employment Rules

Upheld

03 LA 146 04 LA 67 12 LA 350 18 LA 671 24 LA 810 25 LA 709
29 LA 362 30 LA 847 30 LA 94 32 LA 293 44 LA 267 44 LA 772
46 LA 549 47 LA 1029 50 LA 173 51 LA 120 52 LA 764 52 LA 945
58 LA 9 63 LA 355 64 LA 988 67 LA 1296 68 LA 702 70 LA 956
71 LA 329 73 LA 191 74 LA 25 75 LA 90 75 LA 699 75 LA 899
77 LA 1064

Overruled

02 LA 384 10 LA 318 12 LA 386 23 LA 245 27 LA 128 37 LA 130
46 LA 109 48 LA 567 53 LA 1203 55 LA 907 58 LA 546 60 LA 1030
64 LA 742 65 LA 783 69 LA 853 69 LA 1142 74 LA 972 76 LA 1005
78 LA 793

Modified

03 LA 880 09 LA 810 18 LA 400 19 LA 724 21 LA 80 28 LA 829
29 LA 305 29 LA 718 38 LA 1221 39 LA 417 52 LA 405 52 LA 672
52 LA 825 54 LA 145 54 LA 158 55 LA 1274 56 LA 837 56 LA 856
56 LA 860 57 LA 637 58 LA 279 59 LA 292 66 LA 948 68 LA 1230
69 LA 811 69 LA 1071 70 LA 1028 71 LA 613 72 LA 198 74 LA 664
75 LA 255 75 LA 1147 78 LA 141 78 LA 1060

8. Under the Influence

Upheld

14 LA 856 18 LA 671 29 LA 362 30 LA 94 32 LA 293 41 LA 333
55 LA 994 56 LA 738 58 LA 9 59 LA 429 60 LA 159 60 LA 1236
65 LA 723 66 LA 1037 68 LA 421 74 LA 316 75 LA 699 75 LA 899
77 LA 854 77 LA 1064 77 LA 1180

Overruled

12 LA 386 46 LA 109 53 LA 1203 59 LA 329 65 LA 159 65 LA 193
69 LA 853 69 LA 1142 74 LA 972 76 LA 1005

Modified

18 LA 400 19 LA 724 21 LA 80 28 LA 829 29 LA 305 29 LA 718
39 LA 417 40 LA 935 41 LA 987 52 LA 653 54 LA 145 54 LA 158
56 LA 860 66 LA 948 66 LA 1136 68 LA 1230 69 LA 811 71 LA 613
72 LA 198 72 LA 1069 73 LA 1236 74 LA 664 75 LA 255 77 LA 775
79 LA 196

9. Use

Upheld

03 LA 146 10 LA 75 12 LA 350 16 LA 317 28 LA 226 44 LA 267
44 LA 772 46 LA 549 51 LA 120 52 LA 764 52 LA 945 56 LA 1191
59 LA 849 63 LA 355 66 LA 443 70 LA 956 71 LA 329 73 LA 191
77 LA 448 77 LA 1052

Overruled

32 LA 420 35 LA 757 37 LA 130 58 LA 546 65 LA 783 78 LA 793

Modified

09 LA 810 38 LA 1221 49 LA 190 52 LA 405 52 LA 672 52 LA 825
55 LA 1274 56 LA 319 56 LA 837 56 LA 856 57 LA 10 57 LA 637
58 LA 279 59 LA 292 64 LA 829 69 LA 344 70 LA 1028 75 LA 1147
77 LA 289

10. Possession

Upheld

04 LA 67 50 LA 173 68 LA 702 74 LA 25 75 LA 90

Overruled

10 LA 318 23 LA 245 48 LA 567 55 LA 907 75 LA 518

Alcohol, contd.

11. Sleeping on Duty

Upheld

20 LA 50 49 LA 1120 75 LA 896

12. Absenteeism

Upheld

30 LA 163 42 LA 1251 45 LA 769 46 LA 737 49 LA 117 63 LA 618
67 LA 56 71 LA 737 72 LA 355 74 LA 641 79 LA 182

Overruled

15 LA 616 28 LA 434 28 LA 885 56 LA 527

Modified

65 LA 803 71 LA 158 73 LA 1193 79 LA 529

13. Other Disciplinary Infractions

Upheld

19 LA 674 21 LA 367 25 LA 709 37 LA 906 44 LA 308 45 LA 932
52 LA 195 52 LA 435 55 LA 306 60 LA 1335 63 LA 274 67 LA 1145
67 LA 1296 70 LA 756 73 LA 228 75 LA 968

Overruled

14 LA 102 24 LA 173 42 LA 408 55 LA 677 56 LA 789

Modified

34 LA 14 44 LA 1043 59 LA 334 64 LA 477 66 LA 965 67 LA 847
71 LA 445 72 LA 809 73 LA 1185 80 LA 193

14. Off-Premises Misconduct

Upheld

19 LA 674	24 LA 810	30 LA 163	37 LA 906	41 LA 1091	42 LA 1251
44 LA 267	45 LA 769	45 LA 932	46 LA 549	46 LA 737	49 LA 117
52 LA 195	52 LA 1279	56 LA 1191	63 LA 274	63 LA 618	66 LA 443
66 LA 1037	67 LA 56	67 LA 1296	70 LA 756	71 LA 329	71 LA 737
72 LA 355	74 LA 641	77 LA 1052			

Overruled

02 LA 384	14 LA 102	15 LA 616	28 LA 434	32 LA 420	37 LA 130
56 LA 527	56 LA 789	57 LA 637	78 LA 793		

Modified

03 LA 880	38 LA 602	38 LA 1221	41 LA 987	56 LA 837	64 LA 829
65 LA 803	66 LA 948	66 LA 965	68 LA 1230	69 LA 344	71 LA 158
71 LA 445	72 LA 809	73 LA 1185	73 LA 1193	73 LA 1236	74 LA 664

15. Medical and Technical Evidence

Upheld

20 LA 50	30 LA 163	41 LA 1091	42 LA 1251	45 LA 932	48 LA 1187
49 LA 564	50 LA 173	52 LA 764	55 LA 994	56 LA 738	59 LA 849
60 LA 1236	63 LA 274	66 LA 1037	67 LA 1145	68 LA 421	70 LA 956
73 LA 191	75 LA 699	75 LA 968	77 LA 1180		

Overruled

11 LA 195	31 LA 832	55 LA 677	56 LA 527	56 LA 789	60 LA 1030
64 LA 742	65 LA 159	74 LA 972	76 LA 1005		

Modified

28 LA 829	39 LA 417	40 LA 935	52 LA 653	54 LA 145	64 LA 829
66 LA 948	67 LA 847	71 LA 613	72 LA 809	75 LA 255	80 LA 193

Alcohol, contd.

16. Blood Tests

Upheld

50 LA 173 59 LA 849 66 LA 1037 67 LA 1145 68 LA 421 73 LA 191
77 LA 1180

Overruled

31 LA 832 60 LA 1030 76 LA 1005

Modified

28 LA 829 71 LA 613 75 LA 255

17. Breath and Urine Tests

Upheld

29 LA 362 60 LA 1236

Overruled

64 LA 743 74 LA 972

Modified

66 LA 948

18. Refusal to Take or Offer a Test

Upheld

29 LA 362 60 LA 1236

Modified

66 LA 1136 69 LA 811 72 LA 198 72 LA 1069 78 LA 89 80 LA 193

19. Lay Observation

Upheld

03 LA 146	04 LA 67	07 LA 292	10 LA 75	12 LA 350	14 LA 856
16 LA 317	18 LA 671	19 LA 57	19 LA 674	19 LA 733	20 LA 50
21 LA 367	21 LA 452	25 LA 709	28 LA 226	29 LA 362	30 LA 94
30 LA 163	30 LA 847	41 LA 333	44 LA 267	44 LA 772	46 LA 549
47 LA 1029	48 LA 1187	49 LA 117	49 LA 564	49 LA 1120	50 LA 173
52 LA 195	52 LA 435	52 LA 764	52 LA 945	55 LA 306	55 LA 994
56 LA 738	58 LA 9	59 LA 429	59 LA 849	60 LA 159	60 LA 1335
63 LA 274	63 LA 355	64 LA 988	65 LA 723	66 LA 443	67 LA 1145
67 LA 1296	68 LA 421	68 LA 702	70 LA 956	71 LA 329	71 LA 737
73 LA 228	74 LA 25	74 LA 316	75 LA 90	75 LA 699	75 LA 896
75 LA 899	75 LA 968	77 LA 448	77 LA 854	77 LA 1052	77 LA 1180
78 LA 302					

Overruled

02 LA 305	02 LA 384	10 LA 318	11 LA 195	12 LA 386	14 LA 102
18 LA 336	23 LA 245	24 LA 173	27 LA 128	35 LA 757	37 LA 130
41 LA 888	41 LA 1083	42 LA 408	46 LA 109	48 LA 567	53 LA 1203
55 LA 677	55 LA 907	58 LA 546	60 LA 1030	63 LA 1102	64 LA 743
65 LA 159	65 LA 193	65 LA 783	69 LA 853	69 LA 1142	74 LA 972
75 LA 518	76 LA 1005				

Modified

03 LA 880	07 LA 704	08 LA 97	09 LA 810	18 LA 400	19 LA 724
21 LA 80	28 LA 829	29 LA 305	29 LA 718	34 LA 14	38 LA 602
38 LA 1221	39 LA 417	40 LA 717	40 LA 935	44 LA 1043	49 LA 190
52 LA 405	52 LA 653	52 LA 672	52 LA 825	54 LA 145	54 LA 158
55 LA 1274	56 LA 856	56 LA 860	57 LA 10	57 LA 637	58 LA 279
59 LA 292	59 LA 334	64 LA 477	66 LA 948	66 LA 1136	67 LA 847
68 LA 1230	69 LA 344	69 LA 811	69 LA 1071	70 LA 1028	71 LA 445
71 LA 613	72 LA 198	72 LA 1069	73 LA 1185	74 LA 664	75 LA 255
75 LA 1147	77 LA 775	78 LA 1060	79 LA 196		

B. Drugs

20. Employment Rules

Drugs—Employment Rules, contd.

Upheld

56 LA 1191 58 LA 1299 60 LA 1160 62 LA 146 64 LA 404 64 LA 859
64 LA 880 67 LA 773 67 LA 828 68 LA 792 69 LA 776 69 LA 965
70 LA 318 72 LA 11 72 LA 622 72 LA 784 72 LA 1075 73 LA 1133
74 LA 1012 75 LA 301 75 LA 816 76 LA 961 77 LA 721 77 LA 1085
78 LA 545 78 LA 753 78 LA 921 78 LA 1092 78 LA 1104

Overruled

12 LA 386 57 LA 884 60 LA 125 60 LA 183 60 LA 778 62 LA 709
63 LA 1265 63 LA 1289 64 LA 832 65 LA 1291 70 LA 1022 72 LA 780
72 LA 1144 73 LA 304 75 LA 722 75 LA 1081 78 LA 1309 79 LA 1185

Modified

64 LA 721 64 LA 828 65 LA 1203 65 LA 1271 66 LA 286 68 LA 183
69 LA 1243 71 LA 82 71 LA 585 71 LA 685 71 LA 949 72 LA 513
73 LA 1066 74 LA 352 74 LA 953 74 LA 1032 74 LA 1103 78 LA 697
78 LA 1147 78 LA 1299

21. Employee Assistance Program

Upheld

66 LA 273 68 LA 679 70 LA 75 75 LA 896

Overruled

57 LA 884

Modified

74 LA 1032

22. Medical and Technical Evidence

Upheld

18 LA 671 38 LA 891 62 LA 146 64 LA 404 64 LA 859 67 LA 773
67 LA 828 69 LA 379 69 LA 776 70 LA 75 70 LA 1100 72 LA 11
72 LA 622 72 LA 784 75 LA 816 76 LA 961 77 LA 721 78 LA 749
78 LA 1092 78 LA 1104

Overruled

57 LA 884	61 LA 253	61 LA 481	63 LA 1289	65 LA 159	65 LA 1291
69 LA 214	72 LA 517	72 LA 780	73 LA 304	75 LA 722	75 LA 1081

Modified

64 LA 721	64 LA 828	65 LA 1271	66 LA 286	69 LA 1243	71 LA 685
72 LA 1022	78 LA 274	78 LA 697			

23. Lay Observation

Upheld

18 LA 671	58 LA 1299	62 LA 146	64 LA 859	65 LA 1233	67 LA 773
67 LA 828	68 LA 741	68 LA 792	69 LA 776	70 LA 75	70 LA 318
70 LA 1100	72 LA 11	72 LA 784	72 LA 1075	72 LA 1107	73 LA 868
73 LA 1133	74 LA 163	74 LA 1012	75 LA 816	75 LA 896	77 LA 1085
78 LA 749	78 LA 753				

Overruled

12 LA 386	57 LA 884	59 LA 709	59 LA 879	60 LA 125	60 LA 183
60 LA 778	61 LA 253	63 LA 1265	63 LA 1289	64 LA 832	65 LA 159
65 LA 386	69 LA 214	69 LA 985	72 LA 517	72 LA 780	73 LA 531
75 LA 722	75 LA 1081	78 LA 1309			

Modified

19 LA 724	60 LA 1160	64 LA 721	65 LA 1271	66 LA 286	66 LA 547
69 LA 1243	71 LA 452	71 LA 685	71 LA 949	72 LA 513	72 LA 1069
73 LA 1066	74 LA 352	74 LA 953	74 LA 1032	76 LA 144	77 LA 1200
78 LA 697					

24. Refusal to Take or Offer a Test

Upheld

66 LA 273	77 LA 1085	78 LA 749	78 LA 753	78 LA 1104

Overruled

65 LA 1291	73 LA 304

Drugs—Refusal to Take or Offer a Test, contd.

Modified

76 LA 144

25. Searches

Upheld

60 LA 613 72 LA 1075 72 LA 1107 77 LA 721 78 LA 1092 78 LA 1104
78 LA 1334

Overruled

60 LA 183 61 LA 253 63 LA 1265 63 LA 1289 71 LA 949 73 LA 304
77 LA 1001 79 LA 1185

Modified

66 LA 547 66 LA 619 68 LA 183 71 LA 452 74 LA 1103 78 LA 274
78 LA 1147

26. Cases Involving Criminal Charges

Upheld

60 LA 502 65 LA 147 65 LA 1101 68 LA 741 76 LA 387 76 LA 961
78 LA 545 78 LA 597

Overruled

59 LA 879 60 LA 183 60 LA 310 61 LA 253 62 LA 377 63 LA 1265
65 LA 1115 65 LA 1291 70 LA 1022 73 LA 304 75 LA 1081

Modified

66 LA 547 68 LA 183 71 LA 452 72 LA 1022

27. Cases Involving Criminal Convictions

Upheld

38 LA 891 58 LA 148 58 LA 1015 60 LA 613 64 LA 826 68 LA 697
69 LA 379 75 LA 301

Overruled

50 LA 632	70 LA 1208	74 LA 33	78 LA 1311

Modified

57 LA 919	60 LA 430	64 LA 828	68 LA 66	68 LA 72	71 LA 82
71 LA 585	71 LA 685	74 LA 1103	79 LA 65		

28. Undercover Agents

Upheld

62 LA 200	64 LA 404	64 LA 880	65 LA 147	68 LA 697	68 LA 792
69 LA 965	72 LA 1075	74 LA 299	76 LA 387	76 LA 961	77 LA 721
78 LA 921					

Overruled

59 LA 879	61 LA 253	62 LA 709	70 LA 1208	72 LA 1144	75 LA 1081

Modified

60 LA 536	65 LA 1203	74 LA 1032

29. Under the Influence (Illegal Drugs)

Upheld

56 LA 1191	58 LA 148	58 LA 1015	58 LA 1299	60 LA 502	60 LA 613
60 LA 1160	62 LA 146	62 LA 200	64 LA 404	64 LA 826	64 LA 880
65 LA 1101	65 LA 1233	67 LA 773	67 LA 828	68 LA 679	68 LA 741
68 LA 792	69 LA 379	69 LA 776	69 LA 965	70 LA 75	70 LA 110
70 LA 319	71 LA 949	72 LA 11	72 LA 622	72 LA 784	72 LA 1107
74 LA 101	74 LA 163	75 LA 301	75 LA 816	76 LA 387	76 LA 961

Overruled

65 LA 1291	72 LA 517	75 LA 722	75 LA 1081

Drugs, contd.

30. Under the Influence (Legal Drugs)

Upheld

18 LA 671 64 LA 859 73 LA 1133

Overruled

65 LA 159

Modified

19 LA 724

31. Cocaine

Upheld

38 LA 891 68 LA 741 76 LA 387

32. Marijuana (On-Premises)

Upheld

58 LA 1299 62 LA 146 64 LA 404 64 LA 880 65 LA 1233 67 LA 773
67 LA 828 68 LA 792 69 LA 776 69 LA 965 70 LA 318 70 LA 1100
72 LA 11 72 LA 784 72 LA 1075 74 LA 1012 75 LA 816 76 LA 961
77 LA 721 78 LA 545 78 LA 921 78 LA 1092 78 LA 1104 78 LA 1334

Overruled

59 LA 879 60 LA 125 61 LA 253 62 LA 709 63 LA 1289 65 LA 386
72 LA 517 72 LA 1144 73 LA 304 73 LA 531 75 LA 597 75 LA 722
75 LA 1081 78 LA 1309 79 LA 1185 79 LA 1327

Modified

60 LA 536 60 LA 1160 64 LA 721 65 LA 1203 65 LA 1271 66 LA 286
66 LA 547 69 LA 1243 71 LA 685 71 LA 949 72 LA 513 73 LA 1066
74 LA 953 74 LA 1032 74 LA 1103 78 LA 141 78 LA 274 78 LA 697
78 LA 1147 78 LA 1299

33. Marijuana (Off-Premises)

Upheld

56 LA 1191 58 LA 148 58 LA 1015 60 LA 502 60 LA 613 65 LA 1101
68 LA 697 72 LA 622

Overruled

50 LA 632 60 LA 183 63 LA 1265 64 LA 832 65 LA 1291 69 LA 985
70 LA 1022 74 LA 33 78 LA 1311

Modified

60 LA 430 64 LA 828 68 LA 66 68 LA 72 68 LA 183 71 LA 82

34. Heroin

Upheld

64 LA 826 69 LA 379 70 LA 75

Overruled

62 LA 377

35. Hashish

Upheld

62 LA 200

Overruled

60 LA 778

Modified

65 LA 1271

Drugs, contd.

36. Stimulants

Upheld

73 LA 868 74 LA 299 78 LA 921

Overruled

59 LA 709 61 LA 481 70 LA 1208 72 LA 79

Modified

57 LA 919 66 LA 619

37. Depressants

Upheld

64 LA 859 78 LA 597 79 LA 69

Overruled

19 LA 724 69 LA 214

Modified

74 LA 352 77 LA 1200

38. Other Psychoactive Substances

Upheld

64 LA 880 75 LA 301

Overruled

77 LA 1001

Modified

71 LA 585 79 LA 65

39. Abuse of Unknown Substance

Upheld

75 LA 896 77 LA 1085

Overruled

12 LA 386 72 LA 1069

Modified

76 LA 144

C. Alcohol and Drugs

40. Cases Involving Both Alcohol and Drugs

Upheld

18 LA 671 56 LA 1191 75 LA 896 79 LA 69

Overruled

12 LA 386 65 LA 159 79 LA 1327

Modified

18 LA 400 19 LA 724 64 LA 829 72 LA 1069 78 LA 141

Notes

Preface

1. The historical background is recounted in W. J. Rorabaugh, THE ALCOHOLIC REPUBLIC: AN AMERICAN TRADITION (Oxford Univ., 1979).
2. *The Presidential Address: Threats to Arbitration,* PROCEEDINGS OF THE THIRTY-FOURTH ANNUAL MEETING, National Academy of Arbitrators (BNA, 1982), 7.
3. G. Somers, *Alcohol and the Just Cause for Discharge,* PROCEEDINGS OF THE TWENTY-EIGHTH ANNUAL MEETING, National Academy of Arbitrators (BNA, 1976), 117.

Chapter 1

1. H. Milt, *Understanding and Dealing with Alcoholism* (Public Affairs Pamphlets, 1980), 11, 13.
2. *Alcoholism and Airline Flight Crewmembers* (memorandum, U.S. Dept. of Transportation, Nov. 10, 1976).
3. Milt, note 1 *supra,* 16–19.
4. In the airline industry, for example, "years of abstinence" often is a pivotal consideration in medically recertifying pilots with a history of alcoholism. As a rule, two to five years of abstinence are required for recertification, unless a rigorous regime of monitoring and treatment is put into effect. *See* B. Pakull, *Alcoholism and Aviation Medical Certification* in ALCOHOLISM: CLINICAL AND EXPERIMENTAL RESEARCH, Vol. 2 (Jan. 1978), 45–46. Studies suggesting that alcoholics can be trained to engage in controlled social drinking have been challenged vigorously. *See* M. Pendery *et al., Controlled Drinking by Alcoholics? New Findings and a Reevaluation of a Major Affirmative Study,* 217 SCIENCE 169 (July 9, 1982).
5. *Armstrong Furnace Co.,* 63 LA 618, 620 (Stouffer, 1974).
6. *Jehl Cooperage Co.,* 75 LA 901, 903 (Odom, 1980).
7. *Charleston Naval Shipyard,* 54 LA 145, 151 (Kesselman, 1970).
8. *Thrifty Drug Stores Co.,* 56 LA 789, 794 (Peters, 1971).
9. *Armstrong Cork Co.,* 56 LA 527, 529–30 (Wolf, 1971).
10. EMOTIONAL HEALTH AND EMPLOYER RESPONSIBILITY (Cornell Univ., 1966), 25.
11. *Id.,* 27.
12. GRIEVANCE ARBITRATION OF DISCHARGE CASES (Queen's Univ., 1978), 67.

13. SPIRITS AND DEMONS AT WORK (Cornell Univ., 1978), 172.
14. C. Schramm & R. DeFillippi, 70 BRITISH JOURNAL OF ADDICTION 274 (1975).
15. Trice & Belasco, note 10 supra, 25.
16. R. Weiss, DEALING WITH ALCOHOLISM IN THE WORKPLACE (The Conference Board, 1980), 42.
17. J. Simons, *Alcoholism, Drug Abuse and Excessive Absences,* PROCEEDINGS OF THE THIRTY-SECOND ANNUAL NATIONAL CONFERENCE ON LABOR (New York Univ., 1980), 133–34.
18. Personal communication from Thomas J. Delaney, Jr., Executive Director of the Association of Labor–Management Administrators and Consultants on Alcoholism (Sept. 16, 1982).
19. *Eden Hospital,* 56 LA 319, 321–22 (Eaton, 1971).
20. *Land O'Lakes Bridgeman Creamery,* 65 LA 803, 804 (Smythe, 1975).
21. *B. F. Goodrich Chemical Co. and Synthetic Rubber Workers, Local 72* (M. Warns, 1982) (unreported), 8–9.
22. Weiss, note 16 *supra,* 26. Weiss reported that fewer than half of the employers surveyed provided disability benefits to alcoholics who could not be returned to employability after treatment. Such benefits, he found, were controversial: "The problem it creates is how to motivate alcoholic employees to stick to their treatment plan when the worst consequence of failure is retirement with long-term disability benefits. Some of the Conference Board's informants viewed the too frequent use of long-term disability as a dangerous cop-out by both management and the insurer, noting the rapid mortality of alcoholics given such retirement." *Id.,* 27.
23. *Borden's Farm Products,* 3 LA 607, 608 (Burke, 1945).
24. *Chrysler Corp.,* 40 LA 935, 936 (Alexander, 1963).
25. *West Virginia Pulp & Paper Co.,* 42 LA 1251, 1253, 1255 (Abersold, 1964).
26. *Du-Co Ceramics Co.,* 63 LA 355, 356 (Wagner, 1974).
27. Schramm & DeFillippi, note 14 *supra,* 273.

Chapter 2

1. American Psychiatric Association, DIAGNOSTIC AND STATISTICAL MANUAL OF MENTAL DISORDERS, 3d. ed. (APA, 1980).
2. J. DeLong, *Drugs and Their Effects,* DEALING WITH DRUG ABUSE: A REPORT TO THE FORD FOUNDATION (Praeger, 1972), 116.
3. In P. Carone & L. Krinsky, DRUG ABUSE IN INDUSTRY (Charles C Thomas, 1973), 90. There is, it should be noted, a body of work indicating a belief that the pharmacological effects of marijuana are not as easily dissipated as some users might believe.
4. *Id.,* 110.
5. Glue sniffing itself may be an offense, however. In New York state, for example, it is punishable by a fine of up to $50 or up to five days' imprisonment.
6. E. Levin & T. Denenberg, *How Arbitrators View Drug Abuse,* 31 ARB. J. 97, 103–04 (1976).
7. *Dept. of Air Force,* 72 LA 1107, 1109 (Culley, 1979).

8. *Stansteel Corp.*, 69 LA 776, 779 (Kaufman, 1977).
9. *Montfort Packing Co.*, 66 LA 286, 294–95, 297–98 (Goodman, 1976).
10. For a useful discussion of the evidence concerning health effects, see G. Russell, *Marihuana Today* (Myrin Institute, 1980).
11. *Mississippi River Grain Elevator*, 62 LA 200, 202 (Marcus, 1974).
12. *Abex Corp.*, 64 LA 721, 726 (Rybolt, 1975).
13. *S.F. Kennedy-New Products*, 64 LA 880, 884 (Traynor, 1975).
14. *National Steel Corp.*, 60 LA 613, 618 (T. McDermott, 1973).
15. *American Welding & Mfg. Co.*, 60 LA 310, 312–13 (Teple, 1973).
16. *Burlington Northern and United Transportation Union*, Public Law Board No. 2295, Award No. 51 (D. H. Brown, 1980) (unreported), 1.
17. *Burlington Northern and United Transportation Union*, Public Law Board No. 2295, Award No. 21 (D. H. Brown, 1979) (unreported), 2.
18. *National Steel Corp.*, 60 LA 613, 617 (T. McDermott, 1973).
19. *Joy Mfg. Co.*, 68 LA 697, 701 (Freeman, 1977).
20. *Hofman Industries*, 273 AAA 9 (Stulberg, 1981).
21. *Southwestern Bell Telephone Co.*, 59 LA 709, 713 (Kates, 1972).
22. *Kentile Floors*, 57 LA 919, 921 (H. Block, 1971).
23. *City of Taylor*, 65 LA 147, 148–49 (Keefe, 1975).
24. *Michigan Power Co.*, 68 LA 183, 188 (Rayl, 1977).
25. Quoted in Levin & Denenberg, note 6 *supra*, 105–06.
26. *Great Lakes Steel Corp.*, 57 LA 884, 886–89 (Mittenthal, 1971).
27. *Great Lakes Steel Corp.*, No. 72-A-317 (Mittenthal, 1972) (unreported), 2, 5, 10, 11.
28. *Joy Mfg. Co.*, 68 LA 697, 701 (Freeman, 1977).
29. *Smith's Food King*, 66 LA 619, 622 (M. Ross, 1976).
30. *Linde Co.*, 37 LA 1040, 1043 (Wyckoff, 1962).
31. *K.L.M. Royal Dutch Airlines*, 66 LA 547, 553 (Kupsinel, 1975).
32. *Inatco Aluminum Corp.*, 68 LA 66, 67 (LaCugna, 1977).

Chapter 3

1. J. Spencer, *The Developing Notion of Employer Responsibility for the Alcoholic, Drug-Addicted or Mentally Ill Employee: An Examination Under Federal and State Employment Statutes and Arbitration Decisions*, 53 St. John's L. Rev. 659 (Summer 1979). The obligations of federal contractors and grantees under the Rehabilitation Act of 1973 are discussed in R. Weiss, Dealing With Alcoholism in the Workplace (The Conference Board, 1980), 53–54.
2. *A History of Job-Based Alcoholism Programs: 1900–1955*, Journal of Drug Issues 171, 194 (Spring 1981).
3. *The 1982 Report on Drug Abuse and Alcoholism: Report to Hugh L. Carey, Governor of the State of New York* (1982), 58.
4. *Id.*, 59.
5. R. Masters *et al.*, *An Employee Assistance Program for Professional Pilots: An Eight Year Review* (Air Line Pilots Association, 1982).
6. *N. Y. Telephone Co. and Communications Workers* (I. Markowitz, Jan. 14, 1980) (unreported), 5–7, 11.
7. *Id.*, 13.

8. *Id.*, 11–12.
9. *N. Y. Telephone Co. and Communications Workers,* Case Nos. A-79-104, 1-80-140 (Schmertz, Aug. 12, 1981) (unreported), 2–3.
10. *Id.* (Company Brief), 20–21.
11. *State of N. Y. and Civil Service Employees* (Mackenzie, Aug. 13, 1981) (unreported), 8–9, 11, 13.
12. *Carpenter Technology Corp. and Steelworkers* (Beneduce, Aug. 1, 1978) (unreported), 8–9.
13. *Northwestern Bell Telephone Co. and Communications Workers,* quoted in LABOR–MANAGEMENT ALCOHOLISM JOURNAL (May–June, 1973), 27–28.
14. *State of Conn. and State, County and Municipal Employees* (Babiskin, May 2, 1980) (unreported), 8–11.
15. *Boston Gas Co. and Steelworkers* (Horowitz, Aug. 4, 1977) (unreported), 8, 4, 7.
16. *Commonwealth of Mass. and Government Employees NAGE* (Role, Oct. 29, 1981) (unreported), 23–24, 27.
17. *See,* for example, *Armstrong Cork Co.*, 56 LA 527 (Wolf, 1971).
18. Personal communication from J. J. Cohane, Manager, Industrial Relations, Boston Gas Co. (Nov. 17, 1981).
19. *Bethlehem Steel Corp. and Steelworkers* (Strongin, 1980). Reported in *LRR Current Developments,* (BNA, March 25, 1980).
20. *Manhattan & Bronx Surface Transit Operating Authority and Transport Workers* (Kheel, July 6, 1972) (unreported), 2.

Chapter 4

1. F. Elkouri & E. Elkouri, How ARBITRATION WORKS (BNA, 1974), 623.
2. *Some Procedural Problems in Arbitration,* 10 VANDERBILT L. REV. 742 (1957).
3. *Kroger Co.*, 25 LA 906, 908 (1955).
4. *International Harvester Co.*, 13 LA 610, 613 (1949).
5. Note 2 *supra*, 741.
6. *Todd Pacific Shipyards Corp.*, 72 LA 1022, 1024–25 (Brisco, 1979).
7. Quoted in E. Levin & T. Denenberg, *How Arbitrators View Drug Abuse*, 31 ARB. J. 97, 106.
8. *Inland Steel Container Co.*, 60 LA 536, 540 (Marcus, 1973). *See* further discussion of this case under "Evidence From Searches" in this chapter.
9. Being labelled an "addict" is another source of stigmatization. *See* "The Grievant as 'Addict'" in this chapter.
10. *State Univ. of N.Y.*, 74 LA 299, 300 (Babiskin, 1980).
11. *Chicago Pneumatic Tool Co.*, 38 LA 891, 893 (C. Duff, 1961).
12. *Id.*, dissenting opinion (unpublished).
13. *Comco Metal Products Ltd.*, 58 LA 279, 281 (H. Brown, 1972).
14. *Id.*, 281–82.
15. *Champion Spark Plug Co.*, 68 LA 702, 705 (Casselman, 1977).
16. *Issacson Structural Co.*, 72 LA 1075, 1078–79 (Peck, 1979).
17. *Smith's Food King*, 66 LA 619, 625 (M. Ross, 1976).
18. *Braniff Airways*, 73 LA 304, 307–08 (Ray, 1979).
19. *Casting Engineers*, 71 LA 949, 952–53 (Petersen, 1978).
20. *Dept. of Air Force*, 72 LA 1107, 1109 (Culley, 1979).
21. *Id.*, 1109.

22. *General Portland*, 62 LA 709, 715 (Autrey, 1974).
23. *Pettibone Ohio Corp.*, 72 LA 1144, 1150–51 (Feldman, 1979).
24. *American Air Filter Co.*, 64 LA 404, 408 (Hilpert, 1975).
25. *Cerro Corp.*, 69 LA 965, 966 (Griffin, 1977).
26. *Inland Steel Container Co.*, 60 LA 536, 540 (Marcus, 1973).
27. *Bamberger's*, 59 LA 879, 881–82 (Glushien, 1972).

Chapter 5

1. *Hi-Life Packing Co.*, 41 LA 1083, 1085 (Sembower, 1963).
2. *General Felt Industries*, 74 LA 972, 975 (Carnes, 1979).
3. *Holliston Mills, Inc.*, 60 LA 1030, 1037 (Simon, 1973).
4. *Northrop Worldwide Aircraft Services*, 64 LA 742, 749 (Goodstein, 1975).
5. *Kaiser Steel Corp.*, 31 LA 832, 833, 835–36 (J. Grant, 1958).
6. *Tennessee River Pulp & Paper Co.*, 68 LA 421, 429–30 (Simon, 1976).
7. *Capital Area Transit Authority*, 69 LA 811, 815 (Ellmann, 1977).
8. *Tennessee River Pulp & Paper Co.*, 68 LA 421, 426 (Simon, 1976).
9. *Blue Diamond Co.*, 66 LA 1136, 1139–41 (Summers, 1976).
10. *Bi-State Development Agency*, 72 LA 198, 199, 204 (Newmark, 1979).
11. *Capital Area Transit Authority*, 69 LA 811, 815 (Ellmann, 1977).
12. *Southern California Rapid Transit District*, 76 LA 144, 151 (Sabo, 1980).
13. *Bi-State Development Agency*, 72 LA 198, 206 (1979).
14. *Blue Diamond Co.*, 66 LA 1136, 1143 (1976).
15. *General Telephone Co. of California*, 60 LA 1236, 1238–39 (Leventhal, 1973).
16. *Fruehauf Trailer Co.*, 29 LA 362, 366 (Phelps, 1957).
17. *Bethlehem Steel Corp.*, 55 LA 994, 995 (Seward, 1970).
18. *Holliston Mills*, 60 LA 1030, 1037 (Simon, 1973).
19. *Cessna Aircraft Co.*, 52 LA 764, 766 (Altrock, 1969).
20. L. Greenberg, *Intoxication and Alcoholism: Physiological Factors*, ANNALS OF AMERICAN ACADEMY OF POLITICAL AND SOCIAL SCIENCE (January 1958), 22, 27.
21. *General Felt Industries*, 74 LA 972, 976 (Carnes, 1979).
22. *Lockheed Aircraft Corp.*, 28 LA 829, 831 (Hepburn, 1957).
23. *Hayes-Albion Corp.*, 76 LA 1005, 1007 (R. Kahn, 1981).
24. *General Felt Industries*, 74 LA 972, 976–77 (Carnes, 1979).
25. *Sperry Rand Corp.*, 59 LA 849, 850 (Logan, 1972).
26. *Atlantic Steel Co.*, 50 LA 173, 176 (Hebert, 1968).
27. *Burlington Northern Railroad Co. and Machinists*, National Railroad Adjustment Board, Second Division, Award No. 8821 (1981) (unreported), 2.

Chapter 6

1. R. Siegel, *Forensic Psychopharmacology: The Drug Abuse Expert in Court*, 1 DRUG & ALCOHOLISM REVIEW 13–14 (Sept./Dec. 1978).
2. *Day & Zimmermann*, 63 LA 1289, 1293 (Stratton, 1974).
3. *BASF Wyandotte Corp.*, 72 LA 11, 14, 15, 16 (Perry, 1978).
4. *Babcock & Wilcox Co.*, 60 LA 778, 783 (H. Dworkin, 1972).
5. *Combustion Engineering*, 70 LA 318, 318 (Jewett, 1978).

6. *Pepsi-Cola Bottlers of Youngstown,* 68 LA 792, 794–95 (Klein, 1977).
7. *Howmet Corp.,* 60 LA 1160, 1163 (Sembower, 1973).
8. *General Foods Corp.,* 65 LA 1271, 1272 (Maslanka, 1975).
9. *Butler Mfg. Co.,* 64 LA 832, 834–35 (Jacobowski, 1975).
10. Siegel, note 1, 17.
11. D. C. Perry, *Street Drug Analysis and Drug Use Trends 1969–1975* (Part I), PHARMCHEM NEWSLETTER (1977).
12. *Keystone Steel,* 72 LA 780, 783 (Elson, 1979).
13. *Abuse of Legal Drugs Is Cited,* N.Y. Times, Nov. 15, 1982.
14. *Stokely-Van Camp,* 64 LA 859, 860–61 (R. Foster, 1975).
15. 35th ed. (Medical Economics Co., 1981), 561.
16. *Carpenter Technology Corp. and Steelworkers* (Jan. 28, 1982) (unreported), 1–2.
17. *Evansville State Hospital,* 52 LA 653, 655, 657 (Witney, 1969).
18. *United Parcel Service,* 72 LA 1069, 1072–1073 (A. White, 1979).
19. *United Airlines, Inc. and Ass'n of Flight Attendants,* Board No. ORD 56-80 (McKelvey, 1981), 20ff.
20. DRUGS OF ABUSE, 3rd ed. (U.S. Dept. of Justice), Preface, 1.
21. A. J. Bray *et al., Urine Testing for Marijuana Use,* 249 JOURNAL OF THE AMERICAN MEDICAL ASSOCIATION 881 (Feb. 19, 1983).
22. *Compass Steel Division,* 74 LA 352 (Seinsheimer, 1980).
23. *Kentile Floors, Inc.,* 57 LA 919 (Block, 1971).
24. *Hoover Universal,* 73 LA 868 (Gibson, 1979).
25. *Chicago Pneumatic Tool Co.,* 38 LA 891 (C. Duff, 1961).
26. Le Monde, Jan. 24, 1982; reprinted in Manchester Guardian, Feb. 21, 1982.
27. *Crashing on Cocaine,* TIME, April 11, 1983, at 23.
28. Most of those reported so far have concerned employees suspended or discharged for criminal activities. See *Chicago Pneumatic Tool Co.,* 38 LA 891 (C. Duff, 1961); *Morrisania [Hospital],* 68 LA 741 (Turkus, 1977); *N.Y. City Health & Hospitals Corp.,* 76 LA 387 (Simons, 1981); *Hofman Industries,* 273 AAA 9 (Stulberg, 1981). The *Hofman* case was discussed in the text associated with note 20 of Chapter 2. See also "The Grievant as 'Addict'" in Chapter 4 for a discussion of the *Chicago Pneumatic* case.

Chapter 7

1. *Day & Zimmermann,* 75 LA 699, 701 (Sisk, 1980).
2. *Hooker Chemical Co.,* 74 LA 1032, 1034 (Grant, 1980).
3. *Ethyl Corp.,* 74 LA 953, 957 (Hart, 1980).
4. *Hooker Chemical Co.,* 74 LA 1032, 1034 (Grant, 1980).
5. *Ethyl Corp.,* 74 LA 953, 957 (Hart, 1980).
6. *Issacson Structural Co.,* 72 LA 1075, 1079 (Peck, 1979).
7. *Compass Steel Division,* 74 LA 352, 353–54 (Seinsheimer, 1980).
8. *Day & Zimmermann,* 75 LA 699, 701 (Sisk, 1980).
9. *Dept. of Air Force,* 72 LA 1107, 1109 (Culley, 1979).
10. *State Univ. of New York,* 74 LA 299, 301 (Babiskin, 1980).
11. *Missouri Public Service Co.,* 70 LA 1208, 1210 (Yarowsky, 1978).
12. *McDonnell Douglas Canada,* 74 LA 1103, 1106 (O'Shea, 1980).
13. *K.L.M. Royal Dutch Airlines,* 66 LA 547, 550, 553 (Kupsinel, 1975).

14. *Northrop Worldwide Aircraft Services,* 64 LA 742, 750 (Goodstein, 1975).
15. *Id.,* 746.
16. *Northwest Airlines,* 56 LA 837, 842 (Wyckoff, 1971).
17. *Id.,* 838.
18. *Trans World Airlines,* 38 LA 1221, 1223 (Wallen, 1962).
19. *Atlantic Steel Co.,* 50 LA 173, 176–77 (Hebert, 1968).
20. *National Car Rental System,* 75 LA 518, 519 (Zumas, 1980).
21. *Inland Container Corp.,* 28 LA 312, 314 (D. Ferguson, 1957).
22. *General Tire Service,* 52 LA 1279, 1281 (Todd, 1969).
23. *Lamb Glass Co.,* 32 LA 420, 424 (H. Dworkin, 1959).
24. *Cities Service Oil Co.,* 41 LA 1091, 1094 (Oppenheim, 1963).
25. *Lockheed Aircraft Corp.,* 37 LA 906, 908 (T. Roberts, 1961).
26. *American Airlines,* 46 LA 737, 740 (Sembower, 1966).
27. *Green River Steel Corp.,* 49 LA 117, 120 (Chalfie, 1967).
28. *International Pipe and Ceramics Corp.,* 44 LA 267, 268–69 (J. Grant, 1965).
29. *City of Milwaukee,* 71 LA 329, 330 (Maslanka, 1978).
30. *Sterling Drug,* 67 LA 1296, 1297–1300 (Draper, 1976).
31. *Burlington Northern and Transportation Union,* Public Law Board No. 2955, Award No. 1 (Eischen, 1982) (unreported), 2.
32. *Burlington Northern and Transportation Union,* Public Law Board No. 1154, Award No. 1 (D. H. Brown, 1973) (unreported), 1, 3.
33. *Burlington Northern and Transportation Union,* Public Law Board No. 1558, Award No. 11 (H. Weston, 1976) (unreported), 2–3.
34. *Georgia-Pacific,* 72 LA 784 (Vadakin, 1979).
35. *Compass Steel Division,* 74 LA 352 (Seinsheimer, 1980).
36. *Emhart Mfg. Co.,* 63 LA 1265 (McKone, 1974).
37. *Porcelain Metals Corp.,* 73 LA 1133, 1134–35, 1139 (R. Roberts, 1979).
38. *McDonnell Douglas Canada,* 74 LA 1103, 1104, 1106–07 (O'Shea, 1980).
39. *Todd Pacific Shipyards Corp.,* 72 LA 1022, 1025–26 (Brisco, 1979).
40. *Oshkosh Truck Corp.,* 75 LA 722, 723–24 (J. Cox, 1980).
41. *Braniff Airways,* 73 LA 304, 305, 309 (Ray, 1979).
42. *USM Corp.,* 61 LA 481, 483–85 (Stark, 1973).
43. *Rexall Drug Co.,* 65 LA 1101, 1103–04 (G. Cohen, 1975).
44. *Blue Chip Stamps Warehouse,* 58 LA 148, 151 (Kenaston, 1972).
45. *Burlington Northern and Transportation Union,* Public Law Board No. 2806, Award No. 36 (Marx, 1981) (unreported), 3.
46. Burlington Northern Policy No. 14:60:01 (January 1, 1982).
47. *Burlington Northern and Maintenance of Way Employees,* Public Law Board No. 2746, Award No. 12 (Kasher, 1982) (unreported), 3.
48. *Burlington Northern and Transportation Union,* Public Law Board No. 2806, Award No. 36 (Marx, 1981) (unreported), 2–3.

Chapter 8

1. C. Schramm, *Development of Comprehensive Language on Alcoholism in Collective Bargaining Agreements,* 38 JOURNAL OF STUDIES ON ALCOHOL 1405–27 (July 1977).
2. *Id.,* 1408, 1411–12.
3. *Atlantic Steel Co.,* 50 LA 173, 174 (Hebert, 1968).
4. *Id.,* 174.

5. *National Car Rental System,* 75 LA 518, 519 (Zumas, 1980).
6. Schramm, note 1 *supra,* 1406.
7. *Id.,* 1422.
8. *Id.,* 1418–19.
9. *United States Steel Corp. and Steelworkers,* USS-16,796 (D. A. Petersen, 1980) (unreported), 5–6.
10. *United States Steel Corp. and Steelworkers,* USS-10,139 (Witt, 1973) (unreported), 3.
11. *United States Steel Corp. and Steelworkers,* USS-16,894 (Rohlik, 1981) (unreported), 5–7.
12. *United States Steel Corp. and Steelworkers,* USS-16,235 (Das, 1980) (unreported), 4, 6.
13. *United States Steel Corp. and Steelworkers,* USS-17,383 (Das, 1981) (unreported), 7–8.
14. *Porcelain Metals Corp.,* 73 LA 1133, 1138 (R. Roberts, 1979).

Conclusion

1. ALCOHOLICS ANONYMOUS (AA World Services, Inc., 1976), 148.
2. For a useful survey of alcohol treatment methods, see THE EFFECTIVENESS AND COSTS OF ALCOHOLISM TREATMENT (U.S. Congress, Office of Technology Assessment, 1983).

Index

S

T

U

V

W

About the Authors

Tia Schneider Denenberg is an arbitrator who serves on the labor panels of the American Arbitration Association, the Federal Mediation and Conciliation Service, the National Mediation Board and state agencies in New York, New Jersey, Connecticut, Pennsylvania and Massachusetts. She has been a permanent arbitrator in a number of industries, including airlines, entertainment, and health, and in the public sector. She is a member of the National Academy of Arbitrators and serves on the board of directors of the Society of Professionals in Dispute Resolution. A graduate of the New York State School of Industrial and Labor Relations at Cornell University, she is an adjunct extension lecturer for that institution. She has contributed articles and papers to the *Arbitration Journal,* the *Monthly Labor Review* and the *Proceedings* of the NAA, SPIDR and the Industrial Relations Research Association. She was the Program Advisor for the AAA Conference on the Arbitration of Alcohol and Drug Abuse Cases in 1980 and the co-director of the First Oxford University/BNA Symposium on Comparative Industrial Relations, held in Oxford, England in 1983.

R. V. Denenberg is a writer and lecturer who specializes in constitutional and legal issues. Educated at Cornell and Stanford Universities and at the University of Cambridge in England, he served as the United States Supreme Court Correspondent for *Newsday.* He has been a Lecturer in Political Theory and Government at the University of Wales and a member of the adjunct faculty at the Columbia University Graduate School of Journalism. He was an editor on the staff of the Week in Review section of *The New York Times* and still contributes regularly to that newspaper. He is the author of articles in the *International and Comparative Law Quarterly,* the *Modern Law Review* and the *Cambridge Law Journal,* and has written four books, including *Understanding American Politics.* Mr. Denenberg has been the recipient of awards and grants from the Alicia Patterson Foundation, the English-Speaking Union, the American Political Science Association and the Ford Foundation.